grief becomes you

ISBN: 978-0-9742512-9-5

Cover photo by Maya Stein.
Book design by Liz Kalloch.
Author photo by Amy Tingle.

grief becomes you

edited by Maya Stein

with work from

Allison Downey | Amy Tingle | Anjika Grinager | Anne-Claire Bonneau | Annette Januzzi Wick | Brandie Sellers

Candida Maurer | Caren Stewart | Carol Mikoda | Carolyn Sargent | Celeste Tibbets | Chris Gutjahr

Christina Tran | Cynthia Lee | Dana Schwartz | David Rosenheim | Diane M. Laboda | Elisabeth Reed

elizabeth claverie | Ellen McCarthy | Evelyn Donato | Gloria Lodato Wilson | Jennifer Glossop

Jennifer New | Jess Larsen Brennan | Kelly Albers | Laura Hoffman | Lisa Prantl | Lynn Bechtel

Margaret Todd Maitland | Marie Louise St. Onge | Meg Weber | Michelle Harris

Naida D. Hyde | Nancy Gerber | Pamela Graesser | Patricia McKernon Runkle

Rachel Weishaar | Randi Stein | Raye Hendrickson | S. Miria Jo | Sally Hikaka

Sarah Greene Reed | Sarah Kilch Gaffney | Shannon Loucks | Shannon MacFarlane

Sherry Jennings | Sondra Hall | Sue Daly | Susan Vespoli | Tamara Bailie | Tanya Levy

Teri Foltz | Theresa Proenza | Tina Cervin | Victoria Ostrer

In memory of my father, David Ethan Stein
June 19, 1947 - April 4, 2017

FOREWORD

Nearly three years ago my sister died and I was in New Hampshire cleaning and packing up her home. That same week, Maya was in France caring for her father. For me, that week, colors were brighter, sounds were louder, and every exchange with a beloved felt heightened. My focus was honed down to a pinpoint.

That week I also floundered in bigger, deeper, and louder ways than I think I ever have before. Floundering through moments and bumpity-bumping through conversations that I never imagined having. I was clumsy and often clumsily making decisions that I was ill-prepared for, and at the end of each day I would crawl into bed cataloguing the events, the moments, the firsts, and the lasts before falling asleep and waking to a day much the same as the one before.

Grief danced along beside me as I ordered death certificates, looked into how to get rid of a car that's in someone's name who's now deceased (not easy as it turns out), brought tea to my mother who was finding it difficult to stand up for longer than a few minutes, played charades with my niece and nephew, walked in the crunchy snow in the woods behind my brother's house, and went to the morgue to identify my sister's body.

And on the other side of that grief and the things to-do, was an image of a pristine frozen oasis of a pond, ice glistening, smooth as smooth can be, and the sun was shining. And in my imagination, Maya and I were skating on that pond together. Holding mittened hands. Gliding out onto a mirror of ice and laughing at the big feathery plumes of breath escaping from our mouths. We'd skate, always in a straight line across the center, never full-circle around the edge. We'd skate until our thighs were numb with cold and fatigue and then we'd skate some more.

Writing this today, I feel like I'm back at that pond with Maya, and I'm lacing my skates on, but in this scenario she has invited a chorus of voices who've gathered to skate with us. In *Grief Becomes You*, Maya has offered up an oasis where we can find kindred stories, but also find comfort and some small bit of clarity around many of the feelings and much of the clumsiness and confusion surrounding loss.

This book is a place to come and listen to how others are holding their grief—with loose hands or tight against their chests. A place to learn and to be surprised, to nod in agreement or draw in a quick breath of understanding. In this collection, Maya has sculpted not so much a "how-to" as an invitation to turn our gaze forward, eyes open, and quietly skate into all the everythings that come along on any ride with grief.

We are never as prepared as we'd like to be. But really, would any "how-to" book show us the way? I'm not sure of the answer to that question, but what I do know is what Maya has put together in this book gives us the gift of sight and insight, gives us companions for the journey, and brings to light what we are often taught to keep hidden—all the ways that grief becomes us.

–Liz Kalloch, November 2019

INTRODUCTION

I want to tell you about my father. Specifically, the snapshot of us on a Fort Lauderdale beach, me, at two or three years old, aloft on his shoulders, both of us squinting in the sun. He is holding my tiny, doughy feet in his hands. My palms are curved around the sides of his head. We look loose and easy, as if we're sharing the same inside joke. This is a bookend.

I want to tell you about my father. Specifically, his garden on the tiny island he lived on in Brittany, France, in the tiny, 12th-century village of Josselin. How you had to cross two footbridges to get to his old stone house, the River Oust underneath you, sometimes raging, sometimes still. How my dad's enormous dining room window looked out into the wildness of it all, and how a bird would come, daily, to tap at the glass and my father would say "Hello, sweetie," and stand there, waiting, until the bird flew off again. How the beauty of that garden lay in its collision and overlap, in the tumble of species against species, in the joyful abundance and intersection of color and texture. This is a another bookend.

I want to tell you about my father. Specifically, his passion for Renaissance and Yiddish music, the boom of his voice when he sang, the way he looked when he played the piano, as if he'd entered the room of something exquisite and sacred and holy and would be there for awhile. How serious he was when he played, how locked in, as if glued to his seat and the keys and the notes on the page and wherever it was these took him to, and how I would sometimes go upstairs and lie on the carpet in the hallway and listen, and it would feel like he was taking me with him. This is another bookend.

I want to tell you about my father. Specifically, a story about a particular banana cake with chocolate frosting in 1979. There is another story from my great-aunt Ethel's second-floor apartment in Culver City, Los Angeles and another one from Quebec where my dad and I sat side by side on the lip of a water fountain and had a conversation that's followed me for 35 years. There are stories from an Israeli kibbutz and a farm at the end of a dirt road in southern New Hampshire and a bus ride in Cuzco, Peru and another about taking the back roads in the Jamaican highlands and winding up in a cave teeming with bats. There are stories about an acupuncturist in Chinatown and a drive through Joshua Tree National Park and that time we saw Blue Man Group in Las Vegas and a story about a chicken recipe I have recreated countless times. These are more bookends.

I want to tell you about my father, but I can't tell you about my father without also telling you about life without my father. His death is a bookend now, too, a heavy one, marking the precise location where our interwoven narrative—the landscape of 45 years of shared experiences and memories and stories—stops. And for the past two-and-a-half years, the absence of my father has threaded itself through everything.

Grief has become a lens, a prism, a mesh-screened window, far more porous and intangible than a bookend. It has become how I move through and metabolize the world, a filter through which my life is now forever tinted. Grief is an inheritance my father has left me with, a complex richness of feeling that announces its arrival with little or no warning, and can swim idly by or swallow me whole. Sometimes, grief is a wave cresting and crashing; other times it's a feather-light tap. However it appears, and however it lands or lingers, grief has become part of who I am.

It belongs to me. It is my tenderest, most rigorous, most forgiving companion, a frayed edge my heart traces as it beats. Grief is how I have learned to bear my father's absence. And it is the place I return to sit on his shoulders, to rest in a circle of light, to hold his face again, and to feel him there, holding me close, keeping me from falling.

Grief Becomes You is a collection of narratives—in stanzas and snippets, in paragraphs and photographs—surrounding loss. It is a gathering place of stories from nearly 60 contributors from around the country and abroad. It is, I hope, a beginning, an opening, a trailhead, a sign on a map that says "It's okay to be here" and "You are not alone." It is, I hope, a way to help carry these and other losses forward, and to encourage more stories of loss to be shared. I believe the visibility of grief is not just valuable but vital to healing, and I am deeply grateful to those who have entrusted their stories to these pages.

–November 2019

For more information about this collection and to read the full text of the excerpted pieces, please visit www.griefbecomesyou.com.

February 28, 2017

The place my father has chosen to live for the past 15 years is unquestionably beautiful. Everywhere you turn, the phrase "ruin and beauty" is out in full force—you see the exquisiteness of old stone and ancient, muddy earth. Yet there is something richly solid about the rickety buildings and the windblown gardens. Every walk along the streets brings me front and center to a sharp contrast of one thing against another, and the interplay between them. In my father's house, there is a bird that returns daily to a branch outside the dining room window to peck at his reflection. Even he is a kind of contradiction. A creature of flight nevertheless landing for a few minutes to practice his hello against the glass.

It is easy to turn a corner here and find yourself in the middle of a photograph. There's a storybook architecture to this village and I'm spending time in between rain showers and quiet meals and doctors' appointment with my father getting happily lost and found in the cracks between cobblestones, watching and witnessing and wondering and wishing. Sometimes, the sun peeks out from thick clouds for a brief moment, as if to say, "I'm still here." And he is. He is.

a rain filled with shoes

You can buy donuts in Brittany, a 12-pack of miniatures that hold
enough reminiscent sweetness you feel less far from home
than you really are. They call them *beignets* here, and the word
stretches at the back of your tongue, where you'd left it in 10th-grade French class.
Those years you spent learning how Marie would ask Pierre to the movies,
or what to say when looking for a swimming pool in July—the textbook didn't tell you
it would be like this, the somber echo of your steps on wet February cobblestones
in a sodden town cemetery potted with plastic flowers. Is there a phrase you could have learned
for the hope you keep carrying, indignantly, as the sky opens up with its million question marks?
Une pluie remplie de chaussures. A rain filled with shoes, or something like that.

–Maya Stein

Nobody is here

He not only lived here inside this house,
he was this house, in fact remains so even now,
inside this house. When I enter, I enter him, I feel him,
I feel the air move in all directions, I feel him fill
the space like light when I flick the switch.
He is not sad or angry though his body curled up
like burned paper here inside this house.
That night his soul slipped into these walls
as if into the arms of a warm winter coat.
He did not rush off from this weak life
but when I speak to him, there's no answer—he
cannot answer, how can he without tongue and throat?
The murmurs of wind through windows, through
cracks in walls, they soothe me, sometimes fool me
but they are not him; he lives in a world of thought
and thought is a soundless realm.
You might say such silence means nobody's here.
But I feel him as I feel myself
within and around this house.

....

–Ellen McCarthy

Gaze at the photo, into the calm face
next to yours, sunlit moment suspended
in strange substance of time. Forget for a moment.

Then remember.

....

from "Trigger"
–Carol Mikoda

What's hard is remembering the way we were—
how we dove into hard work, taking what came
without worry or fear, knowing we could,
doing what we did.

....

from "In-between Times"
–Diane M. Laboda

Weight Loss

Your bones grow lighter. Inside
the box that glows with unseen radiation,
they lose density, mass, as I move them
from one room into another.
Falling asleep, I see you
on that bed, tube in throat,
wrapped in a white shroud.
But a tree rises up, gentle, silent,
from the mound of ashes in my mind.
We watch *The Fountain* again.
Each fragment I eat
reminds me of bark we laid hands on,
walking through forests of leaves and ideas.

Life may have used you (as it will use me)
but I climb Death like a ladder.

....

–Carol Mikoda

Garland

Grief is a garland around you
in the way you dance in the kitchen
making chocolate cake
one moment and the next

You are on your back tears
shining their way to your earlobes
five months now since your dad died
too young and broken hearted

The way your intuition
unmasked itself those final hours
knowing exactly what to do
how to forgive, when to let go

Today we eat a spring lunch while
a hummingbird drinks from sage blooms
you are not alone in grief, love
though he was left and riven

Your heart is big and holds him now
holds us all and the pain too, pink as a new scar
big as a field of poppies
the purest thing I know

....

–David Rosenheim

Your mother died today.
The clogging in your throat
a strange mix.

There's nothing
to say. I gather
your tears as others
gathered mine.

....

from "Separation"
–Raye Hendrickson

Woodchucks have moved into the foundation
of every outbuilding.
The north trail, home to your vigilance, disappeared
in the weeds at pond's edge. No one else walks it with an eye out
for water snakes.
The biggest tulip poplar, our wedding tree, dropped all its leaves at once.
The lawn chair where you read and napped in the sun
tore its garments, gnashed its metal joints past usefulness.

I, being merely alive, wept but then returned to every day
to clean up the sorrow your leaving had strewn about.

....

from "When You Left Us"
–Carol Mikoda

Grief comes in waves, and without any notice. After a while, grief becomes an old friend you are happy to hear from, reopening the sacred space where the dead are still alive.

I have lost my parents. I have lost my marriage and the home I had built. I have lost my career, my work and my colleagues.

I have lost myself, countless times.

And yet, was there anything that belonged to me in the first place?

....

from "When Grief Strikes"
–Anne-Claire Bonneau

In the Darkness

This
prayer
would
tap
like a
red-
tipped
cane

I bow
before the
mystery of
boundless
grace and
compassion

I gave
over my
precious
mind
to this
slender
rod
and got
each day
a plot
where I
could
place a
single
naked
foot

....

–Patricia McKernon Runkle

The husband of a dear friend died a few days ago.
There is nothing, not even counting to seventeen, that brings any peace.

....

from "Counting Syllables"
–Carolyn Sargent

The mockingbird grieves as much as I

The Perez Brothers arrived even earlier than we'd agreed, eager to get started.
They stood for a long time staring up at the branches,
those arms that had filled my sky for twelve years,
arms that no longer were safe.
They talked quietly among themselves
and then began to work.
The bucket truck, the chain saws, the stump grinder.
It took almost two days.
The constant sound of change.
What once was my horizon is now a mound of oak chips.
It was the reason we bought the house,
it was the last thing she could see from the hospice bed.
And now, she is gone, too.
And now, the view is wide open.

Acorn. Stem. Leaf. Twig. Branch. Limb. Trunk.

Ant. Spider. Butterfly. Nuthatch. Chickadee.

Song sparrow. Bluebird. Cardinal. Mockingbird. Blue jay.

Grackle. Mourning dove. Cooper's hawk. Gray squirrel.

Wind. Rain. Snow. Ice. Sunlight. Shade.

Hope. Shadow. Love.

All are grieving.

All must find new shelter.

The mockingbird grieves as much as I.

....

–Celeste Tibbets

The tiger lilies are back, as they always are every June. A welcome to summer and a bittersweet tug at my heart. They were my mother's favorite flowers, or so I tell myself. She's not alive for me to confirm this assumption. But I know she planted them along the railroad ties holding up the massive dirt hill our house was built upon. Every year they returned. Even after she stopped walking. Even after she and my father moved out. Even after her death. Even now, ten years later.

....

from "Time as a Wrinkle"
–Dana Schwartz

Little Deaths

Our genes are suddenly incompatible, my husband's and mine. Or maybe my eggs have simply expired. Either way, the doctor tells us, "The baby won't survive." If our baby does miraculously make it to 40 weeks and I give birth to him, he won't survive more than two or three days. His chromosomes are a mess, but my doctor makes it clear the choice is still ours. When we ask what the next steps would be, he explains that he will insert a slender rod made of laminaria into my cervix. He tells us laminaria is a type of seaweed that will slowly and naturally cause my cervix to dilate. This will help soften it and allow the doctor's instruments to enter my body to help expel this baby before we suffer anymore. I picture my baby floating in a salty ocean, bobbing along peacefully on the waves. I say yes to the procedure that will end his life safely and compassionately.

In the end, his heartbeat stops just before we arrive at the hospital. His tiny parting gift to us.

Years earlier, when I was in college, a friend asked me to come with her when she had an abortion. We drove from our university to another state where she knew of a Planned Parenthood that would do it legally and safely. The night before her procedure we stayed in a nearby motel. I held her hand as we lay together in the double bed and told her a story as if she were my child. "It's like you have a little tooth that is causing you a lot of pain. You can't survive with the pain inside of you. It will all be over soon." Afterward, she rode in the backseat with her head in my lap all the way back to school. She slept off the anesthesia. I stroked her hair while our friend drove. I think we listened to soft music on the radio. I don't think we talked. I think it was raining.

Every month when I bleed, it is like a little death. I know what grief looks like wrapped in a wad of toilet paper. I stand next to the porcelain toilet every 28 days and think about my baby. I think about the three miscarriages prior to the pregnancy that led to that baby boy. I think about the four dilations and curettages, the scooping and scraping my doctor did to save me some of the pain.

I wonder if the politicians who are voting to take away a woman's right to choose know what it is to remember a friendship that sputtered out because sometimes surviving a trauma together is too painful. Sometimes looking at person who stroked your hair and told you a bedtime story is a reminder of a choice you wish you hadn't had to make, but knew with absolute certainty was the right one. I wonder if they know how sometimes kind hands and the bright lights of a doctor's office can trigger tears even after all these years. How the memories of four babies without graves can be kept in a burlap bag in the back of a desk drawer.

I wonder if they know how grief comes in waves every month like a persistent ocean tide, a heavy green seaweed thrusting itself against shore.

–Amy Tingle

One last bite

Just before life spirals down
into the waiting game bag
for my bird, shot in midair—
it is still summer, the summer before
it all begins to end—he wakes from a nap
and asks for a burger, one crooked wing
reaching up, his hand clawing mine.
Such strength!
Still manhood in it!
(Even the cop who lifts him
from the floor five times last month says so.)
And he scolds, Come on! Help me up!
This impatience hard for me, but I say, ok! ok!
I'm doing the best I can!
Which now I regret; I regret all
my corruptions.
And then my arms wrench under his pits
and lift him as the feral wife and forklift I've become.
I lift, lift, my man's heft, his clots of skin,
his flossy eggwhite hair flying from his head,
until he stands,

wobbles

and shuffles,

a man on a ship rocking in storm

and I drop him into the wheelchair and bend down,

nose to nose to cream the bruises on his cheeks.

I don't see my groom in the eyes

and this drains hope, the blood of life,

from my own body

but his hunger galvanizes so I pull

his bird feet from the floor onto the footrests.

He repeats, I want a burger with everything on it!

How shocking. He has not eaten in days

and now when all is lost, when his mouth

and vital organs are going berserk, he craves life--

one last sweet bite of life—

and so I rush to the door, lay down the ramp

and push the wheelchair

hard and fast over that ramp

because it is a bridge

and we are rolling over water

rising, ever rising.

....

–Ellen McCarthy

Air Lifted

My mother, swaddled in blankets like an Egyptian mummy, is airlifted in a net into the sky from an ocean liner in the North Atlantic. Gale-force winds swing her from side to side. Then she is secured in the rescue helicopter. There is not enough gas to lift my father up after her.

In a hospital in St. John's, Newfoundland, she is in a ward with three other women who are also dying. They will become my best friends. Their husbands and daughters will drive me to the motel and buy me presents from the hospital gift shop and make toast at night for us all.

My father tells me not to come, despite the fact that he, still marooned on the ship, will not be able to get there for several days. "We'll let you know if we need you." he says. My friend Sarah says, "You will never regret it if you go."

My mother opens her eyes and sees me standing at the foot of her bed. She bursts into tears of relief and she cries the only tears I see her cry the month she is dying. We lie together on her hospital bed, in the sunshine, and I rub her legs and her feet and her hands (so like mine). She has made lists of things for us to do: move the harpsichord in the living room to make room for the hospice bed, get a cat for my father. That afternoon of quietly talking and holding each other, with the knowledge of her death present, is crystalline in its odd normality, resonant of thousands of other days spent talking with my mother.

The doctor trusts us with the truth: "She has a rare, almost unknown, cancer of the heart. The tumor has eaten most of it away. It will kill her and it will kill her quickly. If it were me, I would just want to get home." But taking her home would require many days driving and a multi-hour ferry. She is not cleared for a commercial plane. So, in the end, we fly in an air ambulance—a

tiny plane, with two pilots, a paramedic, a nurse, and my father and me, huddled in the corner. My mother, heavily sedated, sips water from a plastic cup I put to her mouth. After the last sip, she turns her face from the cup and kisses my hand.

We take her home to hospice in her house in North Carolina. My sister meets us there.

In the next weeks, I fly to North Carolina, to California, and back to North Carolina. I feel I am in a car wreck where time slows down and every minute feels like an hour. The month is the longest of my life and too short.

I make all kinds of decisions, authoritatively, uncharacteristically so, even overruling my father when I think he is wrong. And the bittersweet thing is that he thanks me for it. To have overcome my fear of disobeying him means I am protecting him now more than he is protecting me. I always communicated with him through my mother. It feels like a threshold to talk with him directly. In losing my mother, I become more his daughter.

My sister and I hold her as she takes her last breath.

My mother carried us all—dying with grace and courage and compassion for others, and with love and even humor. And now we will have to carry on, without her.

....

–Elisabeth Reed

Grief moved in next door. Stepping over my welcome mat. Dragging mud across the welcome mat. It rarely knocks when it comes to visit.

Grief makes itself at home in my home. It comes and goes as it pleases, neither friend nor foe.

Grief wraps its arms around my heart. It can be tender. No longer taking me to my knees.

Grief sits patiently, waiting in the space between endings and beginnings.

I wrote this to no one in particular. Sitting by my mom's bed days before she died feeling isolated in the wordlessness of the experience.

If you placed your hand on my heart could you know what is beyond language?

Brutal honesty. Wrenched wide open. Stripped bare of any protection or pretense. Vulnerable to each detail in each and every moment. "Being" the experience.

Giving permission to each moment to simply be what it is. The sacred grace and impossibility of it. The deep longing for what is leaving. The profound tenderness and connection with what is.

....

–Carol Coal

My mind cannot hold everything
I once knew, and yet it does.
Your bright smile,
the one I see in photos,
ones I took myself, trying to
preserve time, halt leaving, hold
every molecule of you. Yet my mind
cannot hold the taste of you,
so nearly gone.

....

from "We Forget Our Stories, but Our Stories Remember Us"
–Diane M. Laboda

March 3, 2017

Twice now, I've walked through the village cemetery. Like most cemeteries I've been to, it is a peaceful, reverent place. There is both a sense of suspension and gravity here, of lives having met their finale and interred into the earth, but also, because I am still above ground, a certain awareness of the span of the bridge that IS a life before it meets that finale.

At home with my father, I feel the dim tension between those two states. How he holds on with such fierceness to anything that binds him to the normalcies of his life before brain cancer—rolling up his placemat after each meal, for example, or keeping the sugar bowl filled—and at the same time, how he is pulled down by the gravitational forces of his illness—fatigue, disorientation, vision distortion, loss of memory—that prevent the kind of robust attention to these details he's used to. When guests come to visit—as they do, frequently—he offers coffee and biscuits but makes no move to get them. The short walk to the mailbox is painstakingly slow, his hands quivering as they retrieve the contents.

My father keeps his shoes by the door, nested in the same exact place every time. He is a creature of habit, and now that habit includes using an extended shoe horn, because he cannot bend down to tie the laces. I watch him from a slight distance, ready to leap if he stumbles, but he keeps his hand on a nearby bureau and stays upright. Once outside, he walks to the bridge, the one that straddles the island he lives on and the path that leads to the village center. He pauses at the gate. This is as far as he'll go, for now.

unseasonable

On a windowsill in his living room, a bright clutch of petals,
stalwart and stubborn against the glass. The dare they make of my own heart: "Believe."
A neighbor vase could easily have wagged its metaphors, to remind of what's
gone missing. The sting of absence. A life gone phantom. But this is the older instinct,
the call pulse-bearing, and the echo ripe and full of promises that can't—and won't—
be broken, even when they are. I wonder, dimly, how long the blooms will last,
but that is never the point. They have returned in such glorious rebellion, my gaze
turns from its own emptiness, as I hope it always remembers to, even
as the inevitable shedding comes and the final, denuded stalk remains,
carrying the memory of each unseasonable blossom in its bones.

–Maya Stein

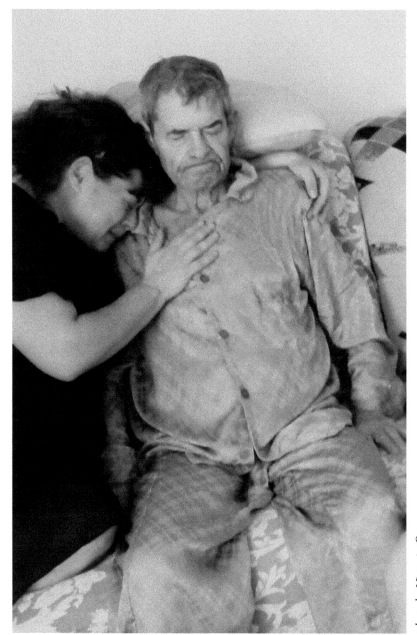

photo by Victoria Ostrer

Instantly

It takes a long time,
it takes many days.
Flurries of movement
follow a long hiatus.
Beside his bed, I crouch,
a beast gauging his stirrings,
looking into the dead-eyed stare of morphine;
smelling its sour vapor.
Holding on to my courage is as hard
as holding onto water.
There are no thunderclaps
but instantly
I know
he will not see another Jack O' Lantern,
another sunrise,
not my face,
not again.

....

–Ellen McCarthy

Timbre and Time

My dad and mom met as young musicians at the Juilliard School of Music—he on the clarinet, she on the flute.

She brought dad home to Sheboygan, Wisconsin. Dad was a Russian Jew from Brooklyn who never bought into the whole God thing. Mom was raised German Catholic in a farming town. These folks had never seen a Jew before. They asked my mom what Jews ate. She said not to go to any trouble. "Just throw on some frankfurters," she said. Word got out. He ate a lot of frankfurters on that trip.

Their marriage was strong. The house was filled with intellectual debate and classical music wafting out of the radio. I remember my parents spending whole afternoons talking about Mozart or listening to cassettes of Glen Gould playing the Bach Inventions. Every Thursday, they would take a bus and two trains from Queens to New York City to watch Zubin Mehta conduct the Philharmonic rehearsals at Carnegie Hall. On Thursdays it was free.

Then my dad got Alzheimer's disease and he couldn't stand to hear music. He couldn't stand sound of any kind. He'd stare, hovering over my mother with his breath held, burning his eyes into the back of her head while she'd heat up some food for him in the cacophonous microwave. She'd patiently explain that the noise would be ending soon. When it was over, he'd turn back around, and sink back into the couch and the quiet.

One fall afternoon, I visit with my husband, Ray. We had been asked to sing at my friend's wedding and came to get some help from my mother with the song "A Nightingale Sang in Barclay Square." Years earlier, this song played as we spoke our vows to each other during our wedding ceremony. For this wedding, we were going to sing it *a capella*, just the two of us. Ray's got the ear for the harmony while I'm always reliable for a steady melody. I knew my mom would be thrilled to help. It would give her a brief rest—a yummy whole note rest—to think about music and not whether my dad was hot or thirsty or what he was trying to say. "No! I want the thing that goes over the other thing and goes *swoosh swoosh* and goes around!" Dad would insist. Mom often looked at me with a mixture of embarrassment and frustration, but mostly a longing for me to help her, to help her make this stop.

The time comes to tell dad the plan for the next hour. "Dad, Ray and I are going to sing at my friend's wedding." He smiles, generally. "Remember when you sang at my wedding and mom played the piano? Remember you sang "Laura"?" "Yeah." He doesn't. They would bicker during rehearsals leading up to our big day. My Mom would chide, "Lee, STOP speaking the lyrics! You're not Tony Bennett!"

But at the wedding, there he was. Tony Bennett in all his glory. In a *sotto voce* lilt, he spoke: "Laura, she's the face in the misty light. Her eyes, how delightful they seem!" Steam emanated from the piano player's ears. All of us were named after their favorite songs. "Danny Boy," "I Dream of Jeannie with the Light Brown Hair." "Laura" was mine.

My mom chimes in: "Lee, Laura and Ray are going to sing now. They're going to be making some noise now." His eyes dart around the room as if he's in trouble. "Lee, do you know what singing is? *La-la-la*—singing. Do you understand what's going on?" My dad suddenly bows his head like someone nodding off to sleep. "No."

"That's okay, honey," Mom continues. "Just come with me into the back room and I'll call you when it's over." She leads my dad's slight frame across the living room, gets him settled in bed and shuts the door behind him. She'd been saying that if she could pick any scenario for the end stages of their marriage, it would be this one. "At least I'm able to take care of him," she'd reason.

She's in the fight of her life. She spends hours at a time screaming in the basement. Dad wants to know what's wrong. What can she say? "I'm upset that you're sick"? And then she's back to making him comfortable, every minute of every day.

When my mom returns to help us, she looks like she's about to eat us alive. She's the abominable snowwoman. Angry, concentrated, her voice is unrecognizable. It startles me at first, but I quickly recognize it as love. Love for music. She is fully channeled.

Ray and I feel silly suddenly, starting tentatively to emulate a nightingale singing. No words yet, just sound. "Oo-oo-oo-oo. . . ." Mom starts talking about taking breaths together and ending breaths together. Work as a team, watch each other, instinctually feel the other's next move. It frightens me to be so intimate, even with my own husband.

Dad opens the door a few minutes into the rehearsal. He walks right past us, not noticing Ray or me, our marriage, our synchronized breathing, our sweet voices. "I don't want this," he says plainly to my mother. I am just noise. How can this be? He used to be so interested in me. He was my champion. Once, when I was 17 and came downstairs to wait for my date, he looked like I had taken his breath away. "You look like a movie star," he said in awe.

Mom explains that it will just be a little while longer, like a dance. She leads him back into the bedroom. "How much more?" he presses. "Soon, honey, just relax now," she says soothingly.

Ray and I continue: Me: "That certain night." Ray: "The night we met." Together: "There was magic abroad in the air . . . there were angels dining at the Ritz, and a nightingale sang in Barclay Square." Just the day before, during a rehearsal, Ray wants to know where the love is in my eyes when I sing to him. He says it seems like I don't even LIKE him. Well, right, because he is too fast here, and too loud there and clumsy with the staging! Why is he letting me down? Why isn't he doing what I want him to do? Why isn't he who I want him to be?

Dad comes out many more times. Each time Mom turns the switch from artist to caretaker. The last time he comes out, she holds him by the shoulders and looks at him in the eyes, their breath intermingling. "I'm going to put you in the car now, honey." She has thought of a way out. She is not giving in. "I DO NOT WANT TO GO IN THE CAR!" each word a staccato mark. I haven't seen a reaction that strong from him, to anything, in years. He looks down and pushes away from her. "Look at me," she orders. She pulls him back so their eyes meet. "We're doing this. You're going to have to stand it." He tries to squirm away, but she doesn't drop him. "Okay, let's go upstairs where it's more quiet. Ten more minutes," she comforts. While she leads him up the stairs, Ray and I stand still, seeing a marriage that is nothing like ours, yet wondering if we are somehow looking into our future. Would Ray be able to see it through like this? Would I?

Mom works with us awhile longer. *Remember to breathe together. Let that phrase happen when you both feel ready, don't rush it. Build this phrase to a crescendo and then let it fade out.* "Is it time yet?" Dad calls from behind the door upstairs. "Not yet, honey," and back to the music. I worry that I would've killed him by now.

When we get to the end of the song, we end with a booming flourish. Mom says the ending needs to be simpler. She takes a gentle phrase from the beginning of the song and adds it onto the end. The new ending is easier to sing. It's more natural. "You already sang this phrase earlier. Now, it's just a memory, a faint echo. . . good. . . quietly. . . shhhhh. Good."

....

–Laura Hoffman

49

I want to write about something other than grief. I could write about the feathery foliage of the trees outside the window, the way the wind moves just the ends of branches, the varying shades of green against the gray sky, the new leaves on the trees behind the evergreens.

I could write about raking off flower beds, the green shoots of hyacinth, daylilies, iris, hosta just barely poking through, the hellebore in full bloom, the epimedium sending up stems that hold delicate pink flowers.

I could write about the pull of muscles in my shoulders, my sore hip carrying me back and forth to the compost pile, my strong-enough back and arms hauling the tarp filled with leaves and sticks, the sun, the breeze blowing hair into my face, the smell of wet earth and composting leaves.

I could write about meditating with friends and the Mary Oliver poem that ends "Finally I saw that worrying had come to nothing/And gave it up. And took my old body/and went out into the morning/and sang."

I want to sing into my life.

I could write about a trip to Andrew's Greenhouse, how the yellow pansies reminded me of sun and I bought a six-pack of those bright blooms to plant out back where I'll see them each morning. I could write about eating lunch at a picnic table, looking at cows grazing, distant hills, sun washing me, pouring deep into me.

Singing into my life.

I could write about the two memorial services I've gone to recently, two friends, talented, vibrant, loving, active women now gone. I could write about going to a concert Saturday night with the partner of one of the women, how he quietly said, "I'm sometimes angry she's not here." I could write about how the music filled and delighted us, how we absorbed the low cello, the viola, the violins.

I could write about my last Christmas with my sister, the small tree under the stairs with white lights glowing, the gold rug, the warm wood of the stair rail, the worn upholstery, the chair that cushioned me, us both laughing at some silly gifts we'd each received.

I could write about the little deaths that accompany us through life, especially through aging, and how those little deaths accumulated in her life, her legs weakening, bones growing fragile, appetite diminishing. I could write about how her house began to feel like a burden rather than a sanctuary. I could write about the loss that accrues from illness and distance and then the final loss.

I think of all the words I've written about my sister so far, her illness and dying, picture the pages and pages printed out and held in my hands. So many words.

But today I want to write about living, about being alive in this rainy, gray world. Today, I want to sing into my life.

....

from "Falcon's Flight"
–Lynn Bechtel

Many Guises

The dialogue of our session starts before I even arrive, flying between us in a flurry of text messages.

I want to say hello before we start today, I write.

Yes, hugs first. Go look at your photo, she answers.

It's one of the rituals we've created for our work. She posts a picture to preview some aspect of the upcoming scene. Today my photo shows three fresh-cut flowers with the caption: *Pain comes in many guises, as does relief.* They don't look sturdy enough to beat me with, so that can't be her intention. I flash on another possibility and then stop wondering. I have to get dressed and out the door so I'm not late.

It's a Monday afternoon six days after my mother's death. The days since have been a chaotic rumble of numbness, relief, and responsibility. The thing that got me through the weekend of funeral planning and parenting my 8-year-old was knowing that Monday would eventually arrive and I'd get to surrender to the mercy of Ma'am's attention.

Now it's Monday and I'm parked outside her house. Typically I wait until exactly the time she expects me before I let myself climb the steps to the wooden porch and knock on the storm door to be let in.

Today I text her: *I'm here early. Can I come in?* I need this too much to make myself wait. She writes back: *Yes.*

She greets me with a fierce hug, tries to decipher how I'm doing. The only specific thing I asked for in today's session was needles—lots and lots of needles.

I hand over the iPod I've loaded with playlists of my favorite sad songs, the ones whose lyrics reverberate in my bones and break me open from the inside. Counting Crows. Cowboy Junkies. Jonatha Brooke.

She pulls me into the center of the room, smoothes her hands down either side of my face, and meets my gaze. Her eyes bathe me in compassion. We are here. Together. For the next two hours I am in her capable hands, held within the brilliant topography of this dynamic we co-create.

She smiles as she takes a seat on the couch. "You know what to do."

When she sits on the floor in front of me, legs crossed, I face her with my back against the couch. I watch her map out the needles she'll use to pierce my chest. Just before each tip breaks through my skin she pauses, tells me to breathe. On my exhale she threads a hypodermic needle through my skin and back out. Sarah McLachlan sings in the background: *Hold on to yourself. For this is gonna hurt like hell.*

Sixteen needles are lined up across my chest. She reaches for the flowers from the photo. She holds up a stem of small purple flowers with a resonant, pungent scent. "This is sage," she says. "It's used for clearing a space, for smudging and healing. I chose it for those qualities, and also because it's purple." She knows purple was my mom's favorite color. She tucks the sprig of sage gently along the needles on the left side of my chest.

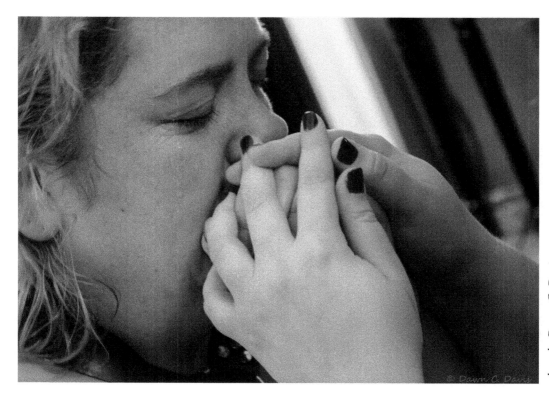

Next she holds up the small orange flower. "Do you know this one?" she asks. I shake my head—even when I'm not high on endorphins from needles, my flower identification skills are shaky at best. "It's calendula," she explains. "Also good for healing. And it's orange." Orange is my favorite color. She knows this, too. She slips it behind the needles on the right side of my chest.

The last flower is a bright yellow dandelion, the color of hope. The lyrics of a song she introduced me to echo in my head. *You were looking for an orchid, and I will always be a dandelion.* She arranges the dandelion at the center of my chest.

She is clearing the room in my heart that houses my grief, a space occupied for the last 14 months by all the emotion surrounding my sister's death by suicide. Now with my mom's death, a new tenant is seeking shelter, a new rush of grief wants to take up residence.

So there, on my chest, above my splintered heart, she has created an altar. She knows the contours of my grief better than anyone. She understands how it lives in my body, knows how to soothe it without pushing it away. She makes room for my sorrow, lends it beauty, decorates it so I can see it shimmer through the threads of my tears.

....

–Meg Weber

Anamnesis

for mothers separated from their children

They say we don't remember
or we would never have another one.
They mean the moment we become a mother
when pressure turns to pain and
the clock ticks slowly, then whoosh
the warm rush streams its way out from inside
through the dark hallway
past all that is open and tender.
The holding, the urge, the sweat,
the howl, the push, the pleasure,
all of it
belongs to the mother.
The moment when precious turns to
violent then back to precious is
the moment the mother is born.
This is never forgotten
no matter where baby is now.

....

–Marie Louise St. Onge

Passage

A pain so sharp, so deep,
pierces beyond the deep.
How can it go deeper
than deep?
But it does.

Opening a hole,
a dark tunnel
a passageway for my sorrow
which flows in and out,
in and out,
bitter and sweet,
sweet and bitter.

Sorrow, waiting to be healed;
but not yet,
for the pain
is the connection.

....

–Sherry Jennings

March 8, 2017

It is strange to wake up and not know if your father is still alive. But he was, recovering from a drainage and a high dose of antibiotics and tucked away in the critical care unit. When I spoke to my wife that morning, she said, "I want to be there with you." And though I knew a part of me could have said, "I'm really okay" and "Stay home" and "I'll be fine," that's not the part that spoke up. "Thank you," I said. And "Yes." And 24 hours later, there she was on the escalator at the Rennes train station.

There has been help offered by so many—friends, neighbors, friends of neighbors, neighbors of friends, both near and far—and it is so clear to me that this is not the time to resist, deflect, or avoid that help. My father once said to me, "You don't have to be a hero"—he was referring to a 1,200-mile bicycle trip from Massachusetts to Wisconsin that I was about to embark on—and in the throes of fear, vulnerability, uncertainty, and the foreign landscape that is the French medical care system (not to mention the language itself)), there is no need to be a hero here either. I am not alone, and I do not need to be alone. And it is both a humbling and expansive discovery, one that connects me so acutely to that other humbling and expansive discovery: love.

It feels like the days are unfolding with a new softness. Like they're being held with the gentlest of hands.

finding your way to Bodieu

I don't know if it helps, but you will know what to do when the time arrives.
Others will give you advice, point you to their own experience. Sorry, there is no video.
Maps are useless. You'll recognize when you've gone too far.
Take a break from your vigil. At the fork of your departure, kiss his forehead.
Remember the sound of the waterfall at the bridge, the weeping willow at the front gate,
the sliding glass door of the village boulangerie. The old cathedral. The cobblestones.
As you leave, you will want to know what happens next, but these things are hidden in the trees.
Later, the plane will level out over the clouds, and you will be looking at an infinity of sky.
This will be one of many signs, like the large green postbox, where his dog greeted you.
He will be looked after. He will be loved until the end.

–Maya Stein

Breathing Lessons

The call that summons me home from a business trip comes as a surprise. After six years of prepping for the other shoe to drop, I drive north in the early morning rain realizing as each mile passes that nothing prepares you.

I arrive to find my mother connected to a large oxygen machine. She is agitated, eyes closed and it is clear she is struggling for breath. Her oxygen level is at 66 and her blood pressure high. A chest x-ray comes back clear.

As I sit with her, she tears the tubing from her nose and I put it back in place only to have her tear at it again. It is a dance we repeat all throughout this day. I swab her lips with water and she seems to like this, pausing in her agitation to suck the last bit of fluid from the swab.

The staff and I talk about her wishes. There will be no antibiotics. The goal is her comfort which includes Morphine. The order has already been written.

They raise her using a Hoyer lift. She no longer assists in her transfer from bed to chair. It is one more reminder this journey has taken a new turn. She does not eat, she does not open her eyes.

I sit mindful of my breath, mindful of hers.… it passes between us.

....

–Pamela Graesser

The World is Full of Doors

Today
the door was rain—
drumming on the roof.
Then, later,
a poem—
which should have been titled
the geography of sorrow.
It spoke of bullets
and children
and death.

I sit here now
in a quiet room
in a sweet house
in a southern New Hampshire town
far from the place
where I knew bullets.
Where a machine gun lived under my bed
and where I learned to aim
and fire.

One day, a bomb fell on our village
and we scattered,
running for shelter.
Death came from above.
Two men succumbed.
One hundred and fifty children lived—
lived in a concrete shelter
for three weeks
a classroom of stunned grief
for the death of those two men—
fathers, husbands, brothers.

No children died that day.
But who knows
how fear can seep into the bones
and turn them to ash
before their time?

....

–Randi Stein

A Geography of Grief

On July 21, 1923, my maternal grandfather was born in a small fishing village in the Bay of Fundy. White Head, so named because of the array of white quartz seen at the head of the island as you approach by boat, is a diminutive, unpresuming place near the more popular and much larger Grand Manan. Just off the coast of Maine and New Brunswick, it is a place of cold waters and much fog.

Ninety-one years later to the day, I am sitting in one of the upstairs bedrooms of the "new" house, built in the late nineteen-teens by the family's best guess, and where my grandmother still lives six months of the year. I am here with my parents and my three-year-old daughter. For them it is a vacation; for me it is a necessity.

Tomorrow marks four months since my husband's death after a long, debilitating battle with a brain tumor. We had a couple of good years post-diagnosis, but the cancer eventually left him bed-bound, unable to communicate, and in excruciating pain. After the longest winter of both of our lives, he died at home on the second day of spring.

This trip is an exercise in escape and relief. It is a reprieve from the size-13 work boots still sitting in the cellar gathering dust, from the piles of clothes to be sorted and donated, and from all of the baby stuff we held onto when there was still hope for another child.

Though she helped me spread some of his ashes at the beach shortly after our arrival here, my daughter is too young to be much of a participant in my own grief, something for which I am often grateful. And though everyone tells me how well I am handling things, I am often overwhelmed with that grief. I am 30 years old and some days it feels like there is nothing right in the world.

White Head has always held a special place in my heart. In an era of families moving about, of a general lack of roots, White Head holds fast for my family. My grandmother has been coming here for 62 years straight. My mother, who spent her childhood summers here, has only missed a handful of annual returns in her life, and I hold the same claim. The first summer my husband and I were together, I brought him to White Head to see the island and meet my mother and grandmother for the first time.

White Head has a year-round population of fewer than two hundred souls, and I am related to a great number of them by marriage or blood. Walking through the island cemetery, I can find the headstone of my great-great-grandmother, for whom I am named. From the house, it is a short walk along the path through the woods to the rocky beach and the enormous tides for which the Bay of Fundy is famous.

The roads are lined with lupines, daisies, and evening primrose. Wild roses abound. The beaches are scattered with stones, shells, driftwood, and sea glass. Crab shells cooked orange in the sun, violet-hued mussels, and a multitude of seaweeds are strewn along the high tide line. Sometimes treasure is washed ashore: moon snail, glass float, seal skull.

On either side of the path to the beach are blue flag, fireweed, and wild blueberries. Spruce and alder are ever encroaching on the path. Beach peas flourish at the sea's edge. There is, of course, great evidence of modern times: bottles, assorted trash, shotgun shells, and brightly colored fishing gear and line, not to mention the pick-up truck someone got stuck (and subsequently abandoned) in the marshy area between Northern Pond and the beach.

There are jagged, rocky outcroppings, sandy inner coves, great expanses of round, tumbled stones. There is peace and quiet and salt in the air. There is a narrow road and sometimes-operational general store. It takes a border crossing and two ferries to get here, and there are no hotels.

For the last decade or so, I have worn a smooth loop of White Head periwinkle shell on a string around my neck. I finger it when I am nervous or uncertain. As a baby, my daughter mouthed it for endless hours, and strangers often inquire as to its nature. It is a small but constant connection to the island.

During our visits to White Head, we disconnect. We walk the dogs on the beach, explore tide pools, and take afternoon naps. We eat my grandmother's fish chowder, read voraciously, and look through old photographs.

This summer, at this moment in time, this is the place I need to be.

Sleeping in the uncomfortable aging bed and my wiggling toddler snuggled close, I fall asleep without reliving my husband's death minute by minute like I do most nights at home. I take several walks a day. I spend time on the beach playing fetch with the dogs, playing hide-and-seek with my daughter, and being by myself. I listen to the waves, finger the smooth stones, and breathe in the salt. I read and knit and eat too many scones.

This afternoon, my grandmother and I will drive in to get the mail and then will proceed to drive all over the island. She will note the inhabitants, current and former, of each house we pass (which I, hopelessly, will not remember half of), and she will provide little bits of historical trivia and local news at every turn. We will pause at the memorial to those lost at sea, then off-road on the old dump road where my grandmother will giggle like a small girl as the car careens off bumps in the uneven path. When we stop to turn the car around, I will find the most beautiful patch of ripe wild blueberries, when all the rest we have come across have still been hard and pale.

Together we will sigh at the beauty of the weirs and of the sea, and as I am still young in her eyes, she will sigh alone at how much has changed and how much is still the same. She will speak of my grandfather, dead these 16 years. She will speak of how everyone here always asks how I am getting along, how this place feels like home to her, and how she is so, so sorry.

Later, my father, daughter, and I will drive to the sandy beach out past the wharf. We will leave our shoes in a pile and walk the beach through the warm sand, blustery wind, and occasional puffs of fog. We will sink our feet in the wet sand at the water's edge and my daughter will run in and out of the waves squealing. We will be the only ones on the beach, and by the time we leave each of us will have found a special stone to carry home. On the way back to the house, we will get popsicles at the general store and eat them, melting deliciously, in the summer sun.

No matter where anyone in my family goes on to live or work or be, we will have White Head. No matter who lives or dies, we will have White Head. You cannot erase history or grief or love, but we will always have this place. We can come here to seek solitude and nourishment and peace. We can come here to seek quiet and family and the healing properties of salt water and salt air.

I will teach my daughter where to pick blueberries and vow to bring her here as often as I can. I will tell her the story of how she helped me spread her father's ashes across the stones and how she paused to wipe the tears from my cheeks. I will remind her how the room she will eventually sleep in was once mine, and was her grandmother's before that. I will show her love of a landscape, beauty even in the harshest elements, and how the land, how a place, how even a battered rock in the middle of the cold ocean, can help us through the deepest grief.

—Sarah Kilch Gaffney

At the beginning, it feels like I had nothing but words. I wrote often. Every day in fact to the people—to his people, to my people. It was the only way to keep my head above water. Now it feels like I have been pulled under and that sounds incredibly morose but that's not what I mean. I think my words have been pulled under. I am existing in another realm.

And that is what it is. Grief transforms.

In January 2013, a young friend of our family took her own life at age 14. Four weeks later, my 27-year-old nephew died from a drug overdose. Whether purposeful or not, we never found out. I was crushed. I painted "Grief Transforming" because I knew that our family, that our friend's family, would never be the same. I sold it for the price of a poem to someone who loved it so much but absolutely did not have the means to pay for it. I told her to make me an offer and she said, *I will write you a poem*. To this day, it is my favorite transaction.

–Cynthia Lee

My sister is alive and each day I grieve the loss of her. We aren't even a full year apart. Thirteen days out of each year we are the same age. I have only been in the world for 352 days without her.

The changes were small at first. Daily texts and phone calls to overanalyze the increase in symptoms. Weekly commitments to new diets and practitioners recommended. A growing list of things to avoid and triggers to watch out for. Until the day she called the ambulance certain that she was dying. They did not agree. Within hours, my sister's independence slipped away.

In the beginning, I kicked into high helper gear. I am a people pleaser at heart and this was my sister. If she needed something I made it happen. I organized movers, friends, cleaners, deliveries, whatever I was asked until I had exhausted my own self. I thought I could to-do list her back to health.

Then I was angry. Convinced she was taking the path of least resistance. Leaving us all to do her hard things while she rested and waited to feel well again. I wanted her to just get up and get better already.

When she was awarded a diagnosis, a piece of my heart shattered. There was not a doctor with an answer. There was not a group of people to even share the same symptoms with. There was only a vaguely understood syndrome that robbed my sister of the ability to get out of bed and care for herself.

I'd love to tell you I was able to move forward with acceptance. But my grief didn't work like that. I swing between anger, despair, and absolute heartbreak for what we have all lost. We've already lost so much. There is a woman disappearing into the shadows of a comfortable bed, in a dim-lit room with a teddy bear as her most constant companion.

I don't know how to walk about in the world forever with this sister-sized hole in my heart.

from "Missing Sister"
–Shannon Loucks

On Being Fully Human

I'm sitting in the waiting room at my doctor's office, something that's become more and more a part of my routine than I'd like to admit. Most days I'm grateful to be alive, despite the numerous health challenges that have consumed me for the past 14 years. Most days I go about the doctor visits, hospital admissions, tests, blood draws, and I.V. infusions as if it was just something I do, like brushing my teeth or taking a shower.

But as I sit here this morning, waiting for my name to be called, I'm feeling a heavy weight on my heart. I pick through the various adjectives, trying to lay claim to the one that fits what I'm feeling. And then I realize what it is. It's grief. Bone-crushing, heart-wrenching grief. Grief for the life I used to have before the diagnosis that changed everything.

I want to lay down my armor and sink into the sorrow. The regret. I want to cry. But of course I don't. And not because there is a room full of people, but because I rarely give myself permission to be vulnerable. Especially around my illness. I soldier on and tell myself I could have it so much worse, or that I'll be letting others down, or that it's self-pitying to allow the negative feelings room to breathe.

This is further complicated by the messages I received as a child. The tape that plays for me says I only receive love and attention when I'm hurt or sick. It's not true, of course, but throughout my life I've let that internalized belief impact my ability to see myself as healthy and whole.

There's been a push-pull relationship with that little girl who got attention the only way she could and the woman who knows I am worth so much more than that. And if I'm honest, there is a residual shame that surfaces when I remember those times I sought out solace, looked for love through the lens of sickness.

I worked hard as I moved into midlife to rid myself of this worn-out tape. Climbed Mount Kilimanjaro at 41 (after more than a year of intense training), cut back on my beloved Mike & Ikes (much more difficult than climbing a mountain), began eating organic fruits and vegetables, making protein-rich shakes and taking probiotics. I thought I'd outrun my past, but life surely loves irony, and at the peak of my 'health' I became seriously ill. Being sick brings up all kinds of vulnerabilities for me.

Shame.

Doubt.

Insecurity.

Self-blame.

In our current culture so much credence is placed on positive thinking and the Law of Attraction and in my work as a coach I've heard my fair share of well-known experts espousing the belief that we bring to our life what we really, truly want. I've even been known to tout these mantras a time or two (or three).

But couched within these well-meaning belief systems is a more insidious message: That if bad things happen, somehow we've asked for it.

The reality is people get sick, bad things happen, and no amount of positive thinking or willing prosperity is going to change that. What we do have control over is how we choose to deal with what life brings to our door.

Sitting in the waiting room, I open up to the understanding that being sick also means I'm human.

I'm human.

And with that understanding, I free the tears that have been aching to be released. I free myself.

....

–Evelyn Donato

Her name is Deirdre. She is Grief.

Deirdre and I are friends, partners, teammates. We are committed to each other.

She requires attention (and sometimes demands it). She has preferences and strengths. She has shortcomings. She is full of quirks and manages to endear me to her regardless.

Some days I devour Deirdre like a crazed stalker. I am head-over-heels into her and suck up everything she does like a sponge. I soak in her. I am awed by her.

Other days I can't stand to look at her. My skin crawls. The delicate skin below my right eye twitches in frustration and maybe even rage that she attempts to be in my life at all. When she comes to visit, I slam the door in her face and scream at her to go away and never, ever return.

Most days I give her an open invitation to come and go as she pleases. I don't fuss about tidying up to receive her. She doesn't comment about the dishes in the sink or the fluffs of cat hair that scurry into the corners. I set a place for her at the dinner table. I invite her to join me in whatever I'm doing. When I am going somewhere where I know her company won't be helpful, I tell her the truth and set boundaries. I let her know I'll be glad to hang out when I finish.

Deirdre listens to what I have to say. She acknowledges my feelings, like the best and most trusted of friends, without judging me. She doesn't chime in with questions about what other things I have tried and have I heard about this thing that her sister's neighbor's boss did because it totally worked. She gives me space to feel what I feel and doesn't rush me. She doesn't move me along because she thinks I should be over something that happened 12 years ago. She knows it hurts, and she knows time doesn't take that away.

She tells me when I'm being impossible. She retaliates when I ignore her. She is one of the best friends I've ever had because she is real and honest every time. She says things that others don't have the courage to say. She is wise. She does not judge me.

She loves me, no matter what.

from "Her Name is Deirdre"
–Shannon MacFarlane

A good friend died four years ago of complications from ovarian cancer. She was 66. We had known each other for 40 years. But we were lucky— her illness progressed slowly, and without much pain, so there was time for me to cherish her, to have her know, really know, how much she meant to me. We had plenty of time to say goodbye.

After three weeks keeping company with her in the hospital, I brought her home to complete her life in the place she loved.

Three days before she died, I wrote: I see today as....a painting, or an orchestral score, full of color and sound and movement. Adrienne dozed, visitors came, and spoke in clusters, quietly or animatedly, or sat with Adrienne at her bedside, or on one of the couches, food was laid on the table and eaten, phones rang and were answered. But that description leaves out the essence of today—the marvelous and inexplicable mix of the ordinary and the sacred, the reverent and the irreverent—Adrienne's hand held gently by each friend in turn (a long turn usually), her feet massaged firmly and lovingly—and a few feet away, sharing of ailments, and news of an evening basketball game, and then, the tender kiss of a nephew on Adrienne's forehead, a hand brushing against her hair. It went on like that all day, the tumble of voices and gestures around Adrienne, the reason we were all here. The list of visitors today is too long to recount, and I know I will leave someone out and feel terrible. Suffice it to say that Natalie, Adrienne's personal care attendant, said she had never seen anything like it in this country, that it reminded her of how things were done in Jamaica, an endless stream of family, surrounding the bed and the room with love—and you could see by the glow on Natalie's face, that this was a very good thing. It was a very good thing.

–Randi Stein

March 12, 2017

Diverticulitis, we were told by his attending physician, a soft-eyed, gentle-voiced German doctor who spoke with us a few days ago. But the confluence of medication involved in my father's treatment—chemotherapy for his glioblastoma, steroids for a subdural hematoma, anti-coagulant for thrombosis in his leg—have wreaked havoc on his platelets, which normally would allow his blood to clot properly and manage infection. So the mathematics of dosages are being carefully adjusted to meet the demand—and limitation—of my father's immunity. This is a necessarily patient process, as each minor, even microscopic, change needs to be observed, noted, and reconfigured if necessary.

Healing is a slow art. The visits with my father reveal small, incremental advances in certain directions, and unfamiliar movements in others. There are rises and dips in energy, attention, and conversation. But there is nothing to do but wait and watch and listen and do my own version of the math, and then, more often than not, to let go of any calculations altogether. There are unseen forces at work—cellular, metaphysical, transcendental. It is an unfamiliar language, but unlike the French I've managed to resurrect for the purposes of my own navigation, there are no words to guide this journey by. There is only surrender.

The hours between visits feel long, and yet at the same time I know that we are all tucking inside of them, away from view, to do our own private work. I can't know the work my father must be doing, on so many levels, but over here on my end of the bridge I have awoken, quite suddenly, to spring. The forsythia are blooming. There is a new greenness along the canal path. The streets are shiny from rain. I feel in the throes of nature's great wisdom, the purposeful turning that marks an ancient and inevitable cycle. There is no clock to tick this passage by, and I am glad for that. There is nothing that needs hurrying. Nothing at all.

how to write about stillness

Not the kind, exactly, of aftermath, though the felled trees
along the riverbank offer instruction of a necessary surrender.
Not the empty seats of a restaurant in the off-season, or the vacancy
of the town square after the circus of the Saturday market,
though their silence hints, importantly, of the narrative that was. The clouds, thick
on this Tuesday morning, appear unmoving, but that's not it either; the forecast
tells otherwise. So what can be said about this brittle skin of vigilance, the hazy tint
washing over these edgeless hours of waiting? My father's garden grows while, in a distant
hospital bed, his hands rest on antiseptic sheets. Each morning, something extraordinary
is taking place, unseen, at the roots of all our lives. Maybe that's something of a beginning.

–Maya Stein

My mother had always been the knot tying our family together. She was an intelligent, industrious, multi-tasker of a woman who could make an ambrosia salad and understood the complexities of Mah-Jongg. If something broke, she fixed it. If something needed to be baked or cleaned, she was ready. There had never been a need for my father to step in—my mother was the human buffer between us all.

Now he was forced to step in. So he worked within his limitations—grilling instead of baking, learning how to wash my mother's clothes, becoming skilled in the application of wigs and scarves, sometimes buttoning up my mother's shirts unevenly—and when it was time to say goodbye, making the necessary arrangements through Hospice. In the end, it was my father's love for my mother that gave me the strength to let her go.

from "Never Say Goodbye"
–Caren Stewart

My Old Purse

I retired my old purse today. It is a large, black leather handbag with a long, over-the-shoulder strap and many pockets. It was my stalwart companion in two battles well-fought but ultimately lost in the past year—my mother's against the ravages of old age and my husband's against cancer.

I no longer need it as my storage system, filing cabinet, and life support, but I can't say goodbye without a few words of appreciation. Its large center pocket held not only my essentials—wallet, hairbrush, and the like—but also my husband's or mother's wallet on those nights when I had to leave one of them in a hospital whose walls carried dire warnings about leaving valuables behind.

My husband's wallet also contained his health card and the blue or green cards for every hospital within a 10-mile radius, a lot of hospitals since we live in downtown Toronto. The main pocket also often carried a book for those long waits for doctors' appointments, tests, or treatments. And when he was in hospital, it was large enough for the daily newspaper, which we shared over his hospital breakfast.

The smaller main pocket held an address book containing the names and phone numbers of all the doctors and all the other numbers and addresses associated with insurers, social services, and friends and family. I learned early on that having these names and numbers at home was not enough. The medical system expects patients or caregivers to have them on the tip of their tongue—along with the names and dosages of all medications now or ever taken.

There were also spare pairs of glasses in this compartment, along with a small Sudoku puzzle book and a pencil for those unexpected (are there any other kind?) trips to emergency when the book got left behind in the rush.

Bottles of medicines also lived in this pocket—a couple of over-the-counter ones, but more importantly, extra pills for when my husband forgot his pain or nausea pills or we were away from home longer than expected.

It also held a flashlight, rarely used, but you never know when the lights will go out.

In the back pocket were the medical records. Here, I kept copies of blood work, CDs of CT scans, and records of prescriptions. Ending up in the wrong hospital without the right records can be a frustrating experience. More than once I walked or drove from one hospital to another to pick up the most recent records. And the prescriptions. They went in that pocket and were dropped off on our way home from the hospital or doctors' appointments to be picked up then or later. Trips to the drugstore were almost daily—so much so that the pharmacist gave us a box of chocolates for Christmas.

This back pocket also served for trips to visit my mother, both the regular monthly trips to look after her finances and household needs after my father died, but also those emergency trips that followed a phone call from a social worker: "Your mother has fallen again. We've sent her to Emergency." The pocket then held airline tickets, hastily purchased, a passport, and a quickly printed Google map to the hospital. On the last of those trips I arrived in time to hold her hand as she breathed her last breaths, surrounded by the caring folk in yet another emergency ward.

I cleaned out the purse before I retired it. In the crevasses, I found an old pair of my husband's glasses and his earring. The glasses had been replaced by newer ones, but the earring had been forgotten. No doubt it had been removed along with his wedding ring and silver bracelet before some medical test or procedure. The wedding ring went into a jewelry box when his fingers became too swollen to wear it, but his silver bracelet stayed with him to the end. I removed it for the last time after he died.

The bracelet is on my wrist now, the papers have been thrown out or filed, and my passport is back in a drawer.

And my new purse? It is smaller and sleeker than the old one, but much emptier and diminished—just like my new life.

....

–Jennifer Glossop

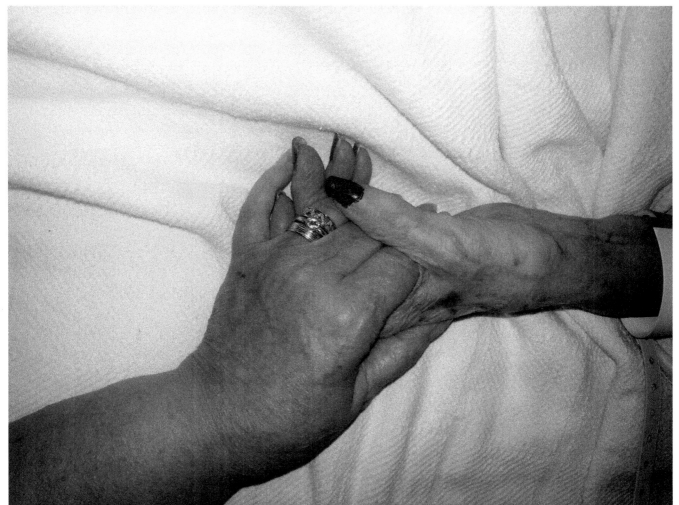

I grasp at my 90-year-old mother's hands from my seat in her old rocking chair while she lies in bed. Her hands are slender, with long nails she once shaped and polished before her Saturday nights out with my father to Pier W for dinner, or at the Italian American Club to hang out with their *compares* and *comares*, or at the movies. Her long feet and fingers are not like my stubby ones. But where once I had added up the ways in which we differed, now that number diminishes.

Our lives have been converging, and I'd never noticed until now.

In her care home, I spoon-feed her pudding and imagine what I had looked like, sick in bed with measles or flu, home from middle school on days when she had stirred up my favorite "get better" concoction—an egg, beaten, with sugar and vanilla. *It's an old Italian thing*, she'd told me once. Some days, I still made this—for the memory, not for the ailment or relief.

Hours ago, the x-rays had been read. My mother had sustained a hip fracture. Serious enough to consider surgery if she were someone else—younger, sprier.

I sign on for hospice care for her instead of surgery for the fractured hip. "It's not end-of-life care," I repeat guiltily to siblings and friends. There was a difference.

In all the decisions I've had to make for my mother, my mother's fall had made the decision for me. Her body was worn down from being worn down.

"I'm here," I remind her and plaster my arms to her torso, unwilling to let go. "We'll get through this together."

Someone turns up the volume on the television in the other room. Dorothy's voice from *The Wizard of Oz* drifts in.

It is the scene where Dorothy first encounters the Wicked Witch of the West after Auntie Em's home lands on the witch's sister. *Just try to stay out of my way,* the witch says. I used to crouch behind the patchwork couch to watch the movie as a youngster, or wrap my skinny arms around my mother's belly and shut my eyes. I can't hide any longer. I have to face my mother and our future. For once in my life, I have to listen to her, and let her make her own way home.

from "Rocking Chair Reflection"
–Annette Wick

He seems taller. Thin, but not skinny. His t-shirt is clean. Gray. He strides in from another room like it hasn't been well over a year since I've seen him. Since I said I wouldn't give him money, and would he please go to treatment. Since he told me I deserted him.

I open my arms and he walks into them. An awkward hug, but still. The top of his scalp shines and is surrounded by a close wreath of stubble.

I like your hair like that.

Adam's girlfriend's 5'6 frame has thinned to 90 pounds yet is velveted in skin a honey-gold. A satin, a sheen. Its luster surprises me. There's a gap where her right lateral incisor and cuspid used to be. She scoops up my daughter's daughter, but Molly squirms free to stand barefoot on the tile and play the plastic pink piano that Adam found in bulk trash.

I ask them about their cat, a pet they love more like a baby.

We have to keep him in the bathroom, so Gibson can't get him. Wanna see?

We all squeeze into the room and close the door to keep my ex-husband's dog out. The cat curls in the sink and looks up at me. Its fur stands up along its spine like a blade.

I watch us in the mirror above the vanity. Hear Gibson whine outside the door. Adam smiles with teeth now the color of ash.

....

from "Fast Forward"
–Susan Vespoli

scattering dad

her sister,
brother,
husband
didn't want to go—

fog looped gray fingers
around the rise in
the valley floor
where she opened the
plastic bag that held
her dead father

she held it up
turned it upside down
dropped out the remains of
a 300-pound taxi driver.
he fell to the ground
in a cloud.

a snake-like mist of
dust rose up from
summer's yellow weeds
just as the morning sun
strode proudly over the hill.

you can't hurt us anymore
was all she said.

....

–elizabeth claverie

Bitter Herbs

Sorrow
steeps the tea.
Mercy sips it.
Regret looks away,
unable to taste
what Sorrow
has brewed.

....

–Sue Daly

The Afterdeath

Cry later. There are chores to be done.
You can almost hear him say it.

First you will need multiple copies of the death certificate -
One is not enough to prove you are an orphan now at 63.
The city clerk will stand at her copier, duplicating your grief.

Locate the will. Go down to the unfinished basement
that scared you when you were small.
Find the dusty filing cabinet near the old furnace.
Pry open the locked drawer with one of his screwdrivers.
When you're finished, put it back where it belongs.

Take the will to the county courthouse
so you can prove you have the right to handle his money—
a fact he always doubted when he lived.
Feel as humiliated as you did in your 20s
when you had to ask for help with your bills.
The clerk will not care.

Stand on a chair to reach the shoe boxes he stacked
on the shelf in his bedroom where he slept alone for ten years.
Gather statements about his life—credit card, banking
mortgage, insurance, tax returns.
Staple his birth certificate to the front of his proof of death.
Bookends of a life.

Notify the post office to stop his mail.
If you don't, it will end up in the dead letter office.
The irony will sting.

Tell the utility companies
that he will no longer need heat or light.

Cancel his memberships.
He no longer belongs here.

Come back to his house where you grew up,
the house where you have been a weekend visitor
for more than half your life.
Heat up one the TV dinners he has in the freezer.
Sit alone at the formica table with your list.
Check off each task.
Make a new list for tomorrow.

Sit on his lumpy couch
and wrap up in the afghan your mother crocheted.
Fall asleep, exhausted.
In a week or two,
when all your chores are done,
cry the cry that will not stop.

....

–Teri Foltz

When my mother died suddenly on March 13, 2018, I thought I knew about grief. I knew I would miss her terribly and I knew my dad and my siblings would, too. I knew I would cry, and that things would never be the same, that holidays would unmoor me. I had friends who had lost parents; my heart had hurt for them, and I had said all the things you say, like, "Please let me know if there's anything I can do for you." I meant it, too, though I knew there's very little anyone can actually DO in times like those. I thought I knew how it would feel when my mom's birthday and Mother's Day and Memorial Day would all fall within the same 30 days. I thought I knew a lot of things.

When we sat in the mortuary choosing flowers for my mom's casket, the funeral director asked me how many calla lilies we wanted for the spray. I said, "Um, I'm not sure. Hold on and I'll ask my..." My voice trailed off. Oh. That's right. The one person who would know the correct answer to that question was the one person I could no longer ask. Because it wasn't really about the lilies.

That was the first of many of those seemingly mundane questions. How does one make the pineapple glaze for the Easter ham just a few weeks after the funeral when Mom isn't there to make it? How does one keep the memory and traditions alive while not drowning in the pressure of feeling that now you have to carry the almost impossible responsibility of doing everything just the way your lost person did it before? The fear of suffering by comparison. And yet I didn't want to feel I was erasing her by not serving pineapple glaze with the Easter ham. So the recipe book was opened, a trip to the store was made for crushed pineapple and brown sugar and cornstarch, and I blinked back tears as I stirred. Because it wasn't really about the pineapple glaze.

My mom died just before the trees were about to get their leaves back. I knew that time would keep passing when she was gone, but what I didn't know was how piercing those visual reminders would be. Each year I looked forward to Spring and all the colors that came back around to replace the dreaded gray of winter. But that year it just seemed unbelievable that time would keep going. Didn't the universe know that I needed it to just pause for a bit? I needed to catch my breath. I needed the world to somehow commemorate this loss. How could the leaves come back to the trees without my mom there to see them? But of course the trees don't wait. Watching the seasons come back around that year almost undid me. Because it wasn't really about the flowers.

I thought I knew about wrapping up the loose ends of someone's life. I had a passing understanding of wills and somehow thought that if you follow the directions in someone's will, it would eventually take care of the steps that must be taken. When my mom's will couldn't be found, the water I was treading filled with lawyers, newspaper notices, and waiting threatened to drown me. And even when the tide went out a bit, a new swell of water flowed in, one filled with possessions: an extensive doll collection, jewelry, figurines, mementos that told the story of a 50-year marriage. How does one distribute tangible reminders of a lifetime without unravelling their collective telling of that story? Because it wasn't about all these things.

I knew that I would not be able to save my dad from his own grief. I just didn't know how to go about the not-saving. I could help him plan the service, I could help him design the headstone, I could bring meals, I could visit, I could invite him on outings. I could help coordinate holiday gatherings and even figure out how to make the pineapple glaze. But I couldn't keep him from his own personal grief. And even though I knew that going in, I didn't know how much it would haunt me.

I knew that I would remember my mom in certain places. My parents' house, of course, but other places, too. What I didn't know is that the recognition would hit me where I least expected it. Warehouse stores became a place where I had to quietly whisper to myself, "It's okay, Tam. You're okay," as I navigated the aisles. Blinking back tears at Costco wasn't what I'd expected when I thought of missing my mom. But how many times had I called Mom and said, "Hey, I'm going to Costco. What do you need?" How many times had I said, "Hey, I saw that Costco put some pretty ribbon out. Do you want me to get any for your wreaths?" Mom always made the prettiest wreaths with the prettiest bows, and she liked to choose when the display first appeared so she had the best selection. That first Christmas without her I froze when I saw the ribbon display and almost had to turn around and go home. So the whispering started. "It's okay, Tam. You're okay." As the months have passed that wave is smaller, but sometimes even now the whispering continues as I make my way through the cavernous store. I didn't know that grief can look like giant packs of paper towels. But it's not really about paper towels.

I knew that I would have mixed feelings when it came to doing things that my mom loved to do. What I didn't know was how those feelings would find me at the strangest times. About a year after she died, we went to Disneyland. I'm fairly certain that no one loved Disneyland as much as my mom. I passed a display of stuffed Mickey Mouses in graduation caps and gowns and tears sprang to my eyes as shoppers bustled around me and I stood perfectly still. Damn. I picked one up and put it in my basket, because I knew my mom would have bought it to give my middle daughter as a graduation present. I looked over at my daughter as she sorted through a T-shirt display, and I thought of how much my mom would have loved watching her graduate. How much my mom absolutely adored my three daughters. What she would have given to be in Disneyland with us all right then. As we took our purchases to the counter, the man helping us check out said, "Oh, a graduate, huh?" And as much as I wanted to say, "Yeah, my mom loved Disneyland, and she loved Mickey, and my daughter is graduating soon and my mom would have absolutely bought her this Mickey Mouse," all I said was, "Yes." So Mickey went into the bag and I blinked hard and handed the clerk my credit card. Because it wasn't really about a stuffed animal.

When my mom died, there were things I thought I knew about grief. Things I thought I knew about living and dying and everything that happens in between. And now that I am a little over a year down that particular fork in the road between the before and the after, I know more than I did before, and one of the things I know is that there are so many things I don't know.

We don't know what day we're on. We don't know what day anyone else is on, either. So I will keep going, in the best ways I know how, and I will keep doing what I can to help other people keep going. Because that's really all we can do, isn't it?

from "It's Not About That"
–Tamara Bailie

March 16, 2017

My father ebbs and flows unpredictably. A few days ago, he tried to yank out one of his IV lines. The next day, he was compliant and positive. Yesterday, he seemed so far away, adrift in a landscape I couldn't recognize or reach, and today, when I walked in, he was moving his legs back and forth and trying to shift positions, as if he were itching to walk. The nurses are trying to get him to eat, but he's not especially interested. He waves them away when they come with their latest offering. There's a window to his left that looks to a distant tree and shows a good swath of sky, and he gazes between there and the clock on the wall to his right. He is keeping time in his own way, I guess.

On my walks before visiting hours, there are flourishes of color everywhere. They are a welcome reprieve from the robotic beeps and buzzes of the hospital, and I am soaking them in like the nourishment they are. I want to bring so many things to my father now—the sound of the water mill just outside the front door of his house, the drape of the willow across the bridge, his morning coffee with a dash of cream, raspberry beignets from the boulangerie down the street, the smell of spring floating down in tiny drops of morning fog, the burst of dandelions everywhere. I think perhaps, even empty-handed, I am carrying these with me on each visit. "This is where you live," I'm saying. "Isn't it beautiful?"

there are fairies in the empty spaces

Good luck charms in the fallen soufflé. A bright, orange balloon
behind the first slippery drafts of a poem. Twinkle lights in loneliness.
Pompoms on the outskirts of bad luck, and caramels underneath the hard shell
of regret. A merry-go-round a few dozen spins away from longing. There are fairies
in the empty spaces, sparklers in the dark, small emerald cities past the heavy,
claustrophobic woods of fear. Even when we think we'll refuse to give up, who can tell me
they haven't fallen to their knees after too many nights of the the heart's weary,
unanswered pleadings? I have wept into that very silence. I have etched my losses
in those walls. And yet, through the smallest of portholes, the air insists.
And then, it is making a bridge. And then, it is holding up the whole sky.

–Maya Stein

The day spreads out in front of you like a map
you cannot read,

angular light piercing through the places where the curtains don't meet.

Don't pick up the framed photograph on the dresser—

the one of her as if no harm could ever come.

But, just like yesterday, you pick it up and stare into her eyes.

She looks so familiar—you recognize that blouse, those silver earrings.

You will not become that smiling woman again.

You will be standing, instead, by the window watching the world wake up,

wondering why grief is the only one who

really knows who you are.

from "Grief is the Only One Who Really Knows Who You Are"
–Sondra Hall

Visitation

Mother stands
the entire time as
the line snakes past
the ache of her feet in
tottering kitten heels
a pain inadequate
to the larger entirety
of suffering.
With each condolence
her shattered face
a tarnished, blotched mirror
reflects the mourners'
fears and denials
that what has happened
can happen to anyone
will happen in the
inevitability of time.
Her lips are pale
as sodden spring worms
that crawl
with a last gasp of hope

from their home of

soil safety

the saturated earth having

expelled them

from what is life-giving and familiar.

Days of wailing and weeping

dries tears to a

dusty sorrow

that settles on her cheeks

and lashes

and permanently inhabits

her eyes.

....

–Lisa Prantl

A Massacre in Christchurch, New Zealand
Friday, March 15, 2019

A response to the slaughter of 51 Muslims at the Al Nur Mosque and the Linwood Community Center by a 28-year old gunman.

One. (1)

8chan. (2)

Magazine. (3)

Jacinda. (4)

Jacaranda. (5)

Manifesto. (6)

Crusades. (7)

Pterodomania. (8)

1. The number of exits in the Al Nur Mosque.

2. Anonymous messaging forum used by the gunman to post his anti-Muslim manifesto and a link for a video live stream of the ensuing slaughter.

3. An illegal MSSA (military-style semiautomatic gun) created by the union of a legal semiautomatic rifle and a legal magazine for 30 rounds of ammo.

4 Jacinda Ardern, Prime Mister of New Zealand, who stated to the gunman, "You may have chosen us, but we utterly condemn and reject you."

5 Jacaranda, the flower celebrated in festivals in Grafton, Australia, population 18,000 and hometown of the gunman.

6 In the words of the gunman, "I am just an ordinary White man… I had a regular childhood without any great issues… I had little interest in education…."

7 The gunman's travels in Europe pre-massacre highlighted obscure sites of Christian-Muslim conflicts.

8 The fern mania of Victorian-era America highlighted in Ligaya Mishan's "In the Beginning: What the oldest plants on earth teach us about surviving turbulent times," *New York Times Style Magazine*, March 24, 2019, pp. 162-164.

....

–Theresa Proenza

I cannot write enough poems
to put my grief to rest.

....

from "In the Foreground of Another Sunrise"
–Carol Mikoda

Kitchen Table

If, suddenly, from the dungeon of death,
he is furloughed
and stands before me.
If, after the swooning shock of his presence
has released me,
my arms will form around him a bird cage,
my face will press into him as into a bouquet
and I will laugh and cry
all at once
because I will not be sure if he is alive
or I am dead.

We will stand there, a vine and trellis.

Eventually, I will say, Come, sit down
at the kitchen table
where every morning he sipped orange juice.

I will wince when I remember
I do not have his favorite jam,
haven't had it since that day.
I will offer to rush to the market
right then and there.
I will offer to bring back everything.

....

–Ellen McCarthy

Still Crying After All These Years

DSM-5

Prolonged Grief Disorder:

Symptoms:

• Feeling that life is empty, unfulfilling and meaningless since the loss

• Confusion about one's place in life; feeling that a part of ones self has died

• Avoidance of reminders of the reality of the loss

• Numbness since the loss

• Diagnosis not to be made until 6 months after the death

A lot can change in nine years. Much can remain the same.

I look over my shoulder to see him following as I walk the hazy streets of Lhassa; I strain to sense his energy in Machu Picchu; I feel his rapid heartbeat as I look into Nelson Mandela's jail cell; I see his smile watching the salt-tipped Iguanas holding hands on the volcanic rock.

But the places are too exotic and dangerous for him. When I wish he was beside me to marvel at sites that seem real and imagined, I know I'm thinking of a man who was never healthy enough. But I imagine him there just the same.

I look into our emptied house. I only take the memories. I look out my new apartment window and see the beautiful sunrise, the turbulent water, the sparkling necklace reflection of the bridge at night. I touch my books and journal articles and see his face looking at me with pride.

I meet another, a widower whose Rubik's Cube has only one square dislodged just waiting for a replacement. I meet another, the man who broke my heart, whose Rubik's Cube center line is all of one color, leaving all others in disarray. I see the Rubik's Cube of my own life; few colors are aligned.

I keep his smiling photograph with our daughter on the kitchen counter, a reminder of how much he loved her. On the back, a different picture of him, in a wheelchair, slumped over, a skeleton of a man, reminding me of how he suffered, hoping to get better to continue our lives as a family. Two cards from him rest hidden within the frame; one says "Just you and Cait matter." The other: "Sometimes I get so wrapped up in myself that I neglect to see your pain. I'm sorry you were so disappointed today."

I feel this undertow, always present, forever pulling and nagging. A constant force to resist for fear of uncontrollably being swept out to the sea, never to return. Swimming straight back to shore never an option; swimming always on a diagonal, hoping to be rescued but continually saving myself.

....

–Gloria Lodato Wilson

my body said,

"Hold on, here's all you're only going to get:
three trips upstairs, one shower,
six phone calls, three trips to the front door
for flowers, a hug, a quiche,
two calls to find your own lost phone
from someone who is no longer there."
Then I must make peace
with the chair in the corner

from *Hitting the Wall*
–Diane M. Laboda

My Father's Stroke

At 2:30 p.m. on September 18, 1995, my father crumpled in a heap and slid off his office chair onto the floor. The staff panicked; they thought he had had a heart attack. Someone phoned Emergency Medical Services, which he refused. My brother arrived and took him to the hospital.

An MRI showed that my father had suffered a mild stroke. But you know how it goes in hospitals: you wait, and you wait, and then you wait some more. Finally, after waiting more than five hours, the hospital found him a bed. It was almost 11 p.m. My father asked my brother to take him to the men's room, where he had another stroke, a massive one, and collapsed on the floor.

When I visit my father the day after his stroke, I am stunned. He is strapped to a flat metal slab in a cubicle of the hospital ICU. He is not in a bed, as I had expected. There is someone else in the room, standing nearby, crying softly: my mother. But I have eyes only for my father. When I last saw him two weeks ago, his sparse circle of hair was gray. Now it is completely white. Even worse is the sight of his immobilized body beneath the sheet that covers him. He looks like the hulk of a ship. My mother leans over and whispers to me that when she saw my father, she nearly fainted.

Every few minutes a nurse comes in and checks his pulse or his blood pressure. "You know, your father is quite a charmer," she says cheerfully. "He's had all of us laughing." There is something comfortingly familiar about that.

"They keep asking me who the president is," says a garbled voice I've never heard before, a voice that comes from my father. "Of course I know who the president is," continues the mangled voice. My head begins to spin. "Yes, Dad," I say, my lips pulled back to form a smile. Perhaps this is what is expected of me, to keep things light, to pretend this is a joke. "Of course you know who the president is." I stumble out of the ICU into the waiting room, where I am told my father's doctors want to speak with me.

By the time the three men in white coats step off the elevator and approach me, I can no longer feel my body. My hands—are they still attached to my arms? I feel as if I am dissolving—literally melting—and I wonder whether the doctors can see this or if I am the only one who knows. Besides, are there really three of them, or is there just one and I'm having hallucinations? Why do they look exactly alike? And what is this they are saying? "Condition very serious. First 24 hours critical. Possibility of cerebral hemorrhage. Not sure of the extent of damage."

I begin to sense their heads bobbing up and down like a chorus of puppets, and my head starts to bob up and down in unison with theirs. Suddenly I have a vision of the four of us standing there in the waiting room, our heads bobbing up and down together, and I nearly laugh out loud. "Thank you, thank you for taking such good care of him," I hear myself say while my hand shoots out to meet theirs.

Like a fleet of small boats, they turn away and enter the elevator. I stand and watch while the gray metal doors close slowly in front of them.

Over the next few days, I develop a new routine: wake up, get the kids to school, cry, go to the hospital, cry, come home, get dinner ready, help the kids with their homework, get them ready for bed, cry, go to sleep.

My father spends three months in institutions: two weeks in the hospital, six weeks at a sub-acute rehab facility, and four weeks in an acute rehab unit. On his last day there his doctor apologizes, saying the paralysis of his limbs is too dense for recovery. There will be no return of mobility in his paralyzed arm or leg. My father will be confined to a wheelchair the rest of his life.

My father lives at home for five years. Five years of loss: the loss of independence, the activities that gave him pleasure—tennis, bridge, movies, concerts, traveling—the loss of his identity as a provider, the loss of his role as an able-bodied companion and spouse, the loss of his ability to play with his grandchildren. It's not just the wheelchair. After the stroke my father's diabetes spins out of control. His short-term memory is compromised. He is weak and easily fatigued. He is extremely depressed.

He is a very sick man.

Then my father loses his battle against diabetes. One day the podiatrist gives him the terrible news: he has gangrene.

My father does not want to have his leg amputated. He says he would rather die of the infection. "Let me die," he says to us.

The doctor tells him gangrene is a gruesome death. It is slow and excruciating, even with morphine. It can take months to die. "The body putrefies," the nurses whisper to my mother. "The stench is awful."

The amputation is scheduled.

My father's leg is amputated on July 20, 2000, my 44th birthday. On the way to the hospital the day of the surgery, my car is rear-ended. I jump out and start yelling at the shaken young woman who hit my car.

At the hospital, my father is in great pain, moaning and thrashing. He cannot take painkillers before the operation.

The minutes tick slowly as my mother and I wait for the attendants to get him. As soon as they place him on the gurney, I rush out of the room, get in my car, and race for home. I do not have the courage to be in the room when my father returns without his left leg.

After the amputation I have nightmares about the missing limb.

"What happens to amputated limbs?" I ask my husband. He says they are disposed of with the medical waste.

The thought of my father's leg being dumped in the garbage is too much. I have visions of finding it and bringing it back to life. When I go to the hospital to visit, I cannot rid myself of the idea that the leg is inside a closet, waiting for me to resuscitate it.

My father stops speaking.

Two months after the amputation, my father goes into a nursing home. The aide at home can't get him out of bed. He does not have the strength to help with transfers from the bed to the wheelchair. It takes two very strong people to lift him, and my mother's osteoporosis means she is not able to assist.

The nursing home looks something like a hotel. The halls are papered in a cheerful red-and-white chrysanthemum pattern, with deep green carpeting to match. If you close your eyes to the people in wheelchairs and the nurses at their stations, you might pretend you are in a Hilton. There is even a tiny coffee shop with a few scattered bistro tables and chairs.

My father likes to be taken to the coffee shop for ice cream floats, which are made with sugar-free ice cream and Diet Coke for diabetic patients like him. He can make that drink last for a good half hour. These outings for ice cream make our visits easier for me, because they give us something to do.

When I visit, I arrive buoyed by a sense of mission and purpose: I am here to do a mitzvah, a good deed: to spend time with my sick father. I am cheered by the silk flowers on the lobby table and the announcement of the week's activities on the bulletin board. "This isn't such a bad place," I say.

But by the time I reach his floor, I am shaken. There is no use pretending that this is some kind of vacation spot. In the dayroom, men and women doze in their metal chairs. From one of the rooms a woman's voice keeps crying, "Nurse, Nurse!" Beneath the sickly sweet smell of antiseptic wafts another odor—familiar, unpleasant, soiled.

I feel guilty all the time.

The women in my support group agree we always feel guilty. Guilty that we aren't always available for our parents. Guilty that we sometimes feel angry with them. Guilty that we want our own lives. Guilty that we can't change anything.

Guilty that we are healthy and they are not.

The group facilitator asks us, "Do you think this guilt is productive? Does it help you become better caregivers?"

We know the answer to these questions, but we feel guilty anyway.

My father has been a resident at the nursing home for nine months when suddenly he becomes very ill. Out of the blue, he spikes a fever of 103; he is delirious and sent to the hospital. The doctors determine that the fever is caused by a staph infection; after a few days of testing, they discover he has sepsis, which cannot be treated with antibiotics and is fatal.

After consulting with the doctors, my father is taken off anything that would sustain life: food, water, insulin, all medications. Even so, he lingers.

It is absolutely wrenching to watch a loved one die. At the end, after all the years of planning, coping, and managing my father's illness, things fall apart. We do not make visitation schedules. Sometimes my mother, brother, and I are there together in my father's room, sometimes one of us is there—sometimes, no one is there. The hours and days creep by slowly.

There is nothing we can do. At first my father is restless and moans, but then he is too weak to do anything. A nurse comes in periodically and adjusts the level of morphine in his IV. Or she gives us washcloths and cups of chipped ice so we can wipe his lips, which are dry and cracked from dehydration. He is not unconscious, but he is too exhausted to speak. It is not a beautiful death.

The days somehow pass. Word has spread that my father is dying and people come to pay their respects. A few hold his hand as they whisper good-bye. My father doesn't open his eyes.

I find myself at the hospital at 6 o'clock one evening. My brother and mother have been there since early morning. I tell them to go home and rest, then I take a seat next to his bed.

I pull my chair over and lift his hand, which is thin and translucent as an onion's skin. "Dad," I say. "Do you know who this is?"

Silence.

"Dad," I press on. "Say my name."

Silence. I am in turmoil, angry at myself for making demands of a dying man, angry at him for what feels like stubbornness.

"Dad, I know you're in there."

Silence. I am about to give up when, out of the blue, I hear, "Nancy."

I am overjoyed that he has made contact. I move even closer and bend my head to meet his. I want desperately to maintain the connection. I can think of nothing meaningful to tell him so I say, "This isn't easy, is it?" And my father whispers, "Nothing is easy."

And then, silence. I know that this silence will be the longest one, that my father will not speak to me again.

And indeed, those are the last words I hear. That evening, shortly after midnight, my father slips into a coma and passes away. We are not there to send him off.

He dies alone.

Years have passed, and I often ruminate on the stroke.

Sometimes I ask myself what I have learned from my father's illness.

I've learned to slow down a bit. I've learned to be less afraid of speaking my mind. I've learned about my own ageism. I'm still learning.

What did my father learn, if anything, from his illness?

That is a more complicated question. He never spoke to me directly of how his understanding of himself changed. He had moved quite suddenly from a place of privilege and dominance within our family to one of powerlessness and invisibility. Even though my life revolved around the stroke for six years, the demands of his illness drove my actions and emotions, rather than my dealings with him and the new person he had become.

I regret that I was not able to get to know my new father.

I took his silences as an accusation; I never understood that what he wanted was companionship, not entertainment. I didn't have to try so hard.

....

–Nancy Gerber
Editor's note: An earlier version of this essay appeared in Illness, Resilience and Spirituality, *edited by Marguerite Guzmán Bouvard.*

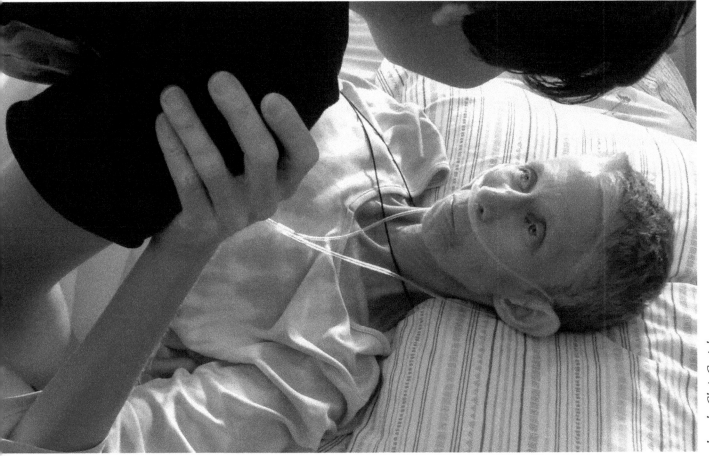

photo by Chris Gutjahr

Knowing

I think I saw the back of your head
in the car in front of me fewer times today.
I think I heard you laugh
at the joke I told a little more faintly today.
Today the phone rang and I think
I knew it wasn't you.
And when I bent over sleeping bodies
tonight to brush my lips over the motionless forms
of my small sons,
I almost didn't see their soft hair
on a satin pillow
in a casket of steel.

I think today I almost know
you're dead.

....

–Teri Foltz

Dear Beloved,

I have been compiling a list of mundane, everyday griefs.

> the loss of a soul
> the killing of a spider (accidental or intentional)
> a miscarriage
> the thinning of seedlings
> wildfires rage
> the spotting of menstruation when one is trying to get pregnant
> the absence of menstruation when one isn't ready for what that means
> the memory of a place we used to call home
> uprootings
> goodbyes

I don't mean to compare sadnesses but I call all of these things griefs in an attempt to connect.

To say: I recognize grief because I know loss.

To ask: How can I help?

Loss is a constant reminder that we don't control everything. Grief is a reminder that life is a dance between what we can do and what happens, what merely is.

I want to stretch out a hand to friends experiencing grief, but I can't quite bridge the distance. No one is as awkward at sending a condolence card to a friend who has lost a parent than one who has previously lost a parent. The news of it reaches you like a vacuum, or maybe in a vacuum—no more breath in this body, no more air in this room. You're supposed to know what to say, but you end up saying nothing.

Instead, I find myself collecting poems I never send, lines that swirl in my mind, like a stainless steel worry ball rolling in one's palm, round and round and round. Wednesday is 15 years since my mom passed.

It is possible that I will experience the fog of grief on Wednesday.

It is possible that I will not.

It is more likely that it will be a random Tuesday, months from now—a childhood plate shattering, or watching the way a mom and her daughter huddle over seedlings, or hearing about the trip of a friend to their grandfather's home—that the weight of loss will roll in.

And if I'm lucky, it will roll back out like an ocean wave, shifting the shoreline, uncovering seashells.

How do we make visible these invisible things?

I imagine a village of yore. A cluster of huts nearby a river, a gather of beings around a fire, everyone knowing everything. The sadness a communal weave resting on the shoulders of the villagers: witnesses all to the cycle of life and death, witnesses all to the one who is in mourning.

Loss is held, and loss is released. More than anything, loss is allowed to flow. It is welcomed with open arms.

We have forgotten these truths. We delude ourselves into believing that anything is ours, that anything is forever, that we suffer. I want to say: I recognize grief because I know loss.

I want to ask: How can I help?

Love,
Christina

....

from "Shifting Shorelines, Uncovering Seashells"
–Christina Tran

I'm at the Tannery Artspace on a mild summer night, holding a space as sacred as birth. A space of mourning. Of shocked and awesome, and fierce and loving grief. It's difficult and prickly, at turns thunderously loud and then velvet silent. Intense and still. And punctuated by healing, cathartic laughter. Or wracking sobs, yelps of pure pain. Chaotic, unpredictable, and raucous.

It is work, but not the kind you'd ever refuse, or ever collect on.

It's as if we've all been suddenly born into a new and terrifying world, illuminated by the lightning shock of something larger than any of us could fathom.

The mother of the deceased is holding court in a humble throne of bent steel and faded upholstery. She is attended by her loving community in a circle of chairs on the concrete courtyard. We are in the corner, opposite the Art Bar, where piles of organic produce have been deposited for the grieving. The flowers and balloons, and the crystals and candles and notes to Maddy are visible through the entranceway. Everyone's teeth are stained purple by donated wine. Maddy's mother is telling poignant and tragic stories of her earlier life, of how we all got here. Or how we might have all gotten here. She describes her own father as a big, bad wolf and her mother as an innocent. But this explanation doesn't hold.

And then she stops. "The Big Bad Wolf. That's who I taught her to fear." And she pauses again.

Maddy loved wolves.

I feel everyone hold their breath for a moment because she tried. She fucking tried and it didn't work. Nobody can explain it and nobody is going to speak up if they can. You don't hold a conversation with a mother during this intense of a transition. You hold space for her, stroke her when she needs it, remind her to breathe, encourage her to get through it. You tell her she can do it. But mostly you just give her the room to do her job of Mother. Even in the sudden terrible, endless absence of Child.

She tried to make sure that Maddy knew what to fear. And it didn't work. Because, in the end, someone at the tail end of childhood himself, cloaked in the lamb's suit of innocence, devoured her only child.

The mother. Laura. She has a name. She was a whole person before Maddy got here. And she'll have to try to be a whole person again now that Maddy is gone.

....

–Anjika Grinager

Scaffolding

I took the dogs out to the marsh;
it's been cold, cold for weeks

and I knew the ice was solid,
but I couldn't leave the edge,
the cattails and grass tufts,
the shallows and alders.

I told myself it was the snow,
the unease of what is unseen:

altered currents and
new soft layers
I might encounter unawares.

It is a terrible thing,
to watch you grow weaker.

It's not that I wouldn't survive
a fall through the ice,
no more than a few feet deep,
and a quarter mile from home,
but I am trying so hard
to keep you.

Our last real conversation
was months ago; some days your
wants and needs escape us both.

No longer partners in this life,
I am your scaffolding;

I can already tell
this will be a long winter,

bitter, and
with slackening belief.

....

–Sarah Kilch Gaffney

I bought peonies today.
They are the color of salmon,
or coral, or fuchsia;
their beauty refuses to be defined.
I snip the ends and place each one
in my favorite teal vase. I become
absorbed into the harmony
of the moment. Soft, fragrant flower petals,
fibrous green stems, delicate, wispy leaves;
together my own private masterpiece.
Gloriously blossoming open,
and dying just the same.

....

from "Peonies"
–Brandie Sellers

Michael's been dead for almost 12 hours when I hear the door open and Kathy is back, her arms loaded. There's a beautiful red silk sari from India and two bolts of silky material from the fabric store, one olive green, one a light cream color. She's also brought a special soap. She says, "We are going to bathe him and wrap him."

She begins to fill a tub with water.

We start the process by stripping off the pajamas he is wearing. Michael's body lies naked and vulnerable on the hospital bed. It's him, but it's not him, and I don't feel embarrassed that Kathy is seeing his body like this.

We get some warm water and the special soap that Kathy has brought with her. I add frankincense to the water and we begin to wipe him down very gently with washcloths and scented water. Since he is lying on his back, we begin with the front of his body. It's stiff and cold, and I find it odd that it's already so dead feeling. But then I realize that this is exactly how it should be.

Kathy begins to wash his genitals. His testicles have been enlarged for almost two years now, and his penis has gradually shrunken into itself until it almost disappears. As we move the testicles aside I see that his skin has been breaking down in the area between his testicles and his legs and it makes me sad. I didn't know about this, and then I realize that he probably didn't know about it either. We gently wipe away the dead skin and I see the raw skin beneath it.

Kathy gets fresh warm water and we turn Michael's body onto its side. As we do, there is a gush of black liquid that pours out of his mouth and nose. We are both taken aback, but Kathy, being a midwife of longstanding, gathers up the sheet, the mattress pad, and the pillow out from under him, and I take them out to the garbage. When I return, she has plugged up his nose and mouth with cotton.

We wipe down his back and his feet and dry him off. Once his body is cleaned we begin to work the red silk sari under him so that it covers the entire bed and hangs down on the sides.

It's hard work moving a dead body that has been beset by rigor mortis, but soon there is a full body wrap of creamy material around him. Already, I can see where we're headed and it's beautiful.

We wrap the olive green cloth under him, around his shoulders, and begin to make a robe-like thing of it. I find an old pillow and wrap it in the same green material and slip it under his head. He looks much better now. Regal, even.

Kathy takes the cotton out of his mouth and nose and gently washes off the remaining black liquid. It's time to build an altar. Michael and I have built many altars over the years to mark important moments, and God knows, this feels most important.

We need to represent the four directions. In Western mystical tradition, East is for Air, South is for Fire, West is for Water, and North is for Earth. We go outside to find some representatives for the elements. The coffee bean tree gives us some unusual brownish-red rattling pods to use, and I grab a black stone and a piece of rose quartz for love.

Fire is easy. I take a red ceramic bowl made by Michael's granddaughter and put a heart-shaped red candle holder in it. For Air I have feathers—beautiful feathers that Michael and I have collected on many of our hikes. I take the eagle feather and the owl feather. I fill a shimmering blue glass vase with water and daffodils for the Water element, and I get more candles. This altar needs to shine.

I begin lighting the candles for the sacred circle, always going clockwise, starting in the East with the color yellow. South is red, West is blue, and North is green. I light a white lotus candle in the center.

It's time to say a few words, words of prayer and peaceful passage, words of gratitude. I am so grateful to have had this person in my life, this beautiful man, this Michael. I already miss him so much. I cry and pray.

Kathy is doing her own thing with prayers and it's clear we both feel the holiness of this moment. We are in the midst of the Sacred, and now is a time for kneeling at the feet of God in whatever way we can. I feel hushed and stilled by beauty. I am filled with awe at the supreme honor of laying out this body for its final end.

The Cremation Society will come at 9 the next morning to take his body away but I know that the real work has already been done. Michael's body has been cleansed and wrapped, his spirit honored, and the Great Powers have been called upon on his behalf. All is well now. All is truly well.

....

from "Laying Out the Body"
–Candida Maurer

March 20. 2017

There is a dead mouse on the path that leads to the bridge that leads to my father's house. I saw him (her?) a few days ago when I left to go to the hospital. The body looked fresh.

My first thought was to move the creature somewhere else—to throw it in the bushes or toss it into the river, which could carry it far away, perhaps as far as Nantes, where the canal ends. The thought was one of dismissal and disappearance—there was part of me that wanted this dead thing out of sight, gone. It felt, in some way, like a twisted harbinger of what could be happening at any moment 10 miles down the road at the hospital in Ploermel, my father already with a clutch of IV tubes coming out of him, continuing his stay in the ICU with its attendant hyper-vigilance and a metronome of beeps and alarms. He was certainly not out of the woods. And yet he seemed to be accepting each piece of not-so-great medical news with a surprising lack of concern.

Each day, as I pass the dead mouse, I see new changes afoot. Flies were the first to arrive, a host of them feasting on the now-exposed intestines. Then it was ants, lifting and carrying what they could, and after the ants, a coterie of other insects consuming the remainders. On visits to my father, I look at the machines and medications being activated in service of prolonging his life, and I am wondering what cost these interventions carry. I suspect one has to find a way to transcend these assaults, and my father has done it beautifully, simultaneously drawing into himself and also peering out, beyond the medical armory being summoned. I imagine him at the lip of a wide green field where everything is quiet and still and whole, and he's wondering how long it will take until he finally is free to enter.

After a week, the little grey-white mouse is almost gone. His death, it turns out, has fed a community of creatures that have paused in their daily journeys to take nourishment. How this small life lies motionless on the path as dozens of teeming lives surround it, and are fed. I am watching my father persist, despite—or perhaps because of—the odds against him. His chest rises and falls. He moves his toes and bends his knees. He opens his eyes and reaches for my hand, and the squeeze he gives is surprisingly firm. Maybe he's not ready to go, or maybe he is. I can't tell. But there is only one thing to do: squeeze back.

improbable auguries

It's like he's here, in these woods, overseeing the proceedings of our short hike
to the falls. Nearby, a set of tires, a burnt-out microwave, the rusty skeleton
of a bike frame, a full bottle of iced tea, frayed remnants of a dog leash, and I wonder
who else has passed by on this trail, paused before these improbable auguries, and known
the tenderest certainty of company. In the parking lot, a single black sock,
sandy with loose gravel, will meet the next traveler, remind her of that day
her mother, now long gone, saved her from a fall in an unkempt river,
and how the wind snatched up one of the pair and sent it to the ether. Now,
it's back, landed at the foot of a rear car door, and she will feel those same hands
wrap her shoulders, tugging her out of the water all over again.

–Maya Stein

I wonder how it was for Dr. House when she leaned down to say, "I'm sorry, but I think it's cancer." I was giddy from the anesthesia, distracted by her dangling gold cross sparkling under florescent lights. The hemorrhoid she removed was not a hemorrhoid, but—cancer? It was hard to piece together. When Dr. House leaves the room I turn to my husband, John: "Why do I have to get ass cancer? Why couldn't I get a respectable cancer like everyone else?" Full belly laugh. When the drugs wear off, confusion. Remembering. The familiar sinking feeling, tightness in my chest. Grief walks in step with my absence around every corner of my life. And sometimes its rage explodes violently inside me, ripping me apart at the baby-toothed smile of my boy in his Batman pajamas. It is that I am the bearer of Grief that I cannot bear. Two days later Dr. House must know this, on the other end of the phone with the biopsy results. A mother herself, voice fragile, shaking, cracking. "I'm sorry. It's just so rare. I'm so sorry. It's just so rare."

....

from "Hard to Bear. Hard to Share."
–Allison Downey

I have left you other love notes
but they won't be as clear
as that crescent moon, waning,
or the earth scent
during mid-winter thaw,
blue sky after weeks of gray clouds,
two notes from a bird in the woods,
the song of water
rippling over the spillway,
the sun's heat on the chimney stones
in the wind-sheltered corner
where we played our guitars.

....

from "Other Love Notes"
–Carol Mikoda

Grief. I have been on a pilgrimage with her. It is both a reverent and chaotic journey. I carry along a walking stick to aid me up the difficult terrain of this process. Grief is like a stone I found along the rocky path. Sometimes round and smooth. Sometimes cracked and uneven. Occasionally, the stone is marked with with beautiful swirls of color and unusually shaped designs. Still others are marked with delineating lines which signal the "before" and "after" of my voyage. I pick each one up and put them in my pocket.

–Kelly Albers

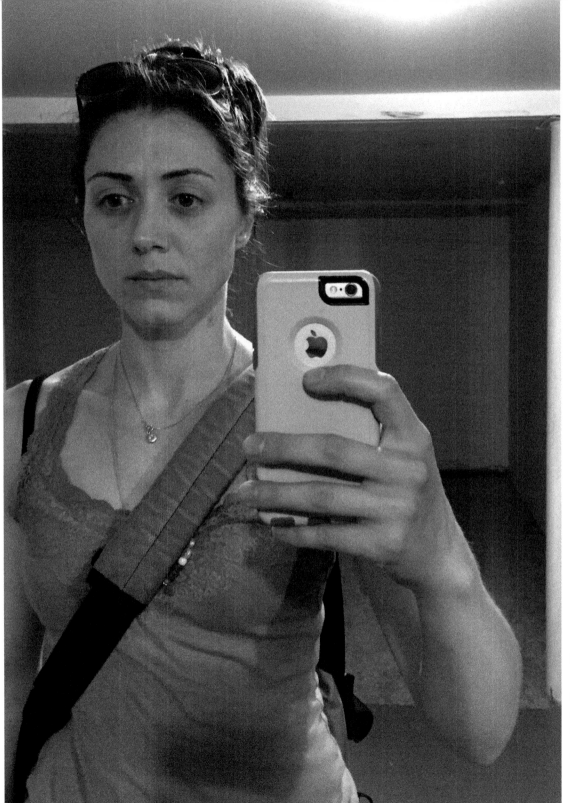

photo by Jess Larsen Brennan

This is a selfie I took three years ago and until now haven't shared with anybody.

I took it as I was about to walk out of my home for the very last time, alone and moving into a new life as a divorced person and a single mother.

I look at it now and notice so many things: the empty basement behind me that had been our family room, where I had folded mountains of laundry and watched movies with my young daughter. A messenger bag that held my passport, wallet, important documents, and computer—the barest essentials, things I couldn't afford to lose. The conspicuous absence of wedding rings on my hand. A beaded necklace my daughter made for me that hung on a doorknob in what had been her bedroom. Mostly, I see how broken I was.

A divorce isn't just the death of a marriage. In the quick division and purge of all of our family's belongings and props, there was the death of a future I'd imagined for all of us, and the accompanying loss of friendships, extended family, a job, a community—so much was lost. In this photo I see my shame, guilt, and the full weight of the empty house around me. There had been so much life and love in that home, and I killed it. (Or so it seemed, then.)

I must have needed to look all that loss squarely in the face. There was so much pain—I was only pain, animate and embodied. But there was something else too, a thing without speech, and it compelled me to simultaneously do an honest accounting of the debris while trusting whatever was tethered to my core and pulled me onward, forward, in a hopeful and loving way. Grace, I can only imagine. And so, for reasons I can't fully explain, I wanted to remember that day and I snapped a photo on my way out.

There's so much to tell about what came after that moment: I found that bereavement literature—widows' words—were my own too, even though my former husband was alive. I learned to companion myself and become a doula for my own grief, and then how to hold space for others going through their own losses. Three years later, I've used all of it to inform a massage therapy practice that specializes in working with people who are grieving.

But none of that was alive when I took this photo.

I was actively standing in the shock of grief, of what had happened, of what was happening. I'd never felt so raw, not during the birth of my daughter, and not amid the death of family members. I was attending the death of my life as I knew it.

I wish I could go back in time and kiss that version of me on the forehead, hug her into my chest and let her weep until she fell asleep. We all deserve a love like that.

....

–Jess Larsen Brennan

We used to dance here

We used to dance here in this living room,
Swoops of ecstasy, eye to eye, heart to heart.
We danced all the way to our bed.
There were ebullient waltzes and disjointed rumbas.
Cranked up high: the Doobie Brothers, Talking Heads, Louis and Ella.
Dances of wounded hearts and broken bones
Dances of wonder and questioning.
Reels, mazurkas, fox trots
The hustle, the twist, the time warp.
Rain dances when quenched,
Ghost dances when abandoned.
We used to dance right here until
You scribed your name on another's card,
She cut in, no permission asked.
A body slam, the mosh pit, a head jerk.
Dancing out of here, into there.
Today, in a sunny room where flowers bloom against the frigid windows,
I dance alone. Dancing with memories of all those other dances.
A dance of gratitude. A dance of sorrow.
I dance it now, right here in this room. Dhikir, the Sufi dance of listening and remembering.
Each step gliding, stuttering into the arms of the first partner: Impermanence.

–Jennifer New

Gone. For you.

My eyes hurt from crying. Some days they hurt from holding it in. It has only been six weeks since I found out your secret, and yet I have continued to make the same mistake for these past several days. I keep thinking I'm done with the sad part now.

I'll get a few hours of respite from grief, and I will think to myself, now I'm to the anger part. Or now I'm on the other side. Then someone says something or I'm reminded because of something you said to me or some truth in the world triggers a realization of how I failed to give myself the life that I intended. Or, like tonight, some friends confess their own sins and start fighting right in front of me even though they should know better, and I'm wrecked once again.

A couple weeks in, after I poured my heart out to you and begged you to stay, I felt my insides scooped out, like a shovel emptying my gut. It was the same as giving birth. I was hollowed out.

And then heartache. It had just been a word, a concept in songs. But I felt the physical pain of my heart aching, pulling me both inward and outward at the same time. And it ached. It hurt so bad.

Now it's the ebb and flow of sorrow and confusion. How could you do this?

Ten years ago I told you that my bucket was empty. Now I'm just shattered. There's no bucket.

The person I loved was a fiction, made up partly of your nice qualities and partly of the man I thought you could become. You are not even my friend.

I will get the whole of me back. Lovely and Vivacious is not gone for good. I hid her in a room down a corridor that I know how to find. I am too tired right now to go there and dust her off and rehabilitate her atrophied muscles. Crying is exhausting and I am not done yet. But I will be. I will get to the other side at some point. And when I do, I will walk down that hall and open the door and she will dance again.

–Michelle Harris

I'm impatient for healing. I imagine
my way forward. My body has had other ideas.

I've come to embrace my daily meltdowns—
the cleansing tears, embodied hurt, a communing
with photos of his sparkling happy eyes.
Even in his dire illness, he strove to live
a meaningful life.

....

from "Inspired Stillness"
–Diane M. Laboda

Crab Apple
-for Dan 1951 - 2018

I don't think I can bear the blooming.

Outside our bedroom window
the buds will burst,
sweet atmosphere of petals and bee pollen
drifting through the air we shared.
Every May our love turned easy.

What's the point now? Dear buds, please forget
to open. Lock up your perfume.
I don't want your subtle invitations.
There will be no sunlit afternoons,
no rising up so light
we floated out the window
to breathe among the blossoms
where all was blessing.

....

–Margaret Todd Maitland

Grief

Grief is a room, invisible.
   You are pushed into it.
      For a while, it is the only
         room in your house.

You stumble around.
   No lights. No clocks.
   No windows.
      Empty.

When darkness is dark enough—
   enough!—you cross
      the threshold, return
         to the visible world.

Dust on your desk,
   on the fruit bowl.
      Kitchen. Remember to eat.
         Living room. Agree to talk.

When dust chafes
   your living skin,
      you'll step outside.
         Sun and wind will be at play

and you'll find yourself smiling.
   Really, I mean find yourself—
      you've been lost all this time.

You have the whole place back now,
   but that room will always be there,
      and the door will always be open.

....

–Patricia McKernon Runkle

Helga: A Love Poem

Scottish plaid nightshirts in sturdy flannel her usual bed attire.
Now she lies shrunken, frail, her parchment skin alabaster
in old lady nighties, tiny pale blue florets patterned on white.

A friend asked yesterday if I would be writing her obituary.
Who else? I answered. How is it possible to distill
her essence into words on a page, not accomplishments
so much as who she has been as she strode the earth
not suffering fools gladly; her struggles, her triumphs,
what made her guffaw, what lit her on fire?
Intimacy from our 32 years, easy to answer.

There is no one else. She shared more than one third
of her days on earth with me, as I have with her, in
admiration and love, soul connection since first meeting
at that long ago Christmas party I dreaded attending,
forcing myself, saying it is good to get out, it will be good for you.
And so it was.

....

–Naida D. Hyde

Yes, he was mine, but he belonged to all of us.

Every time I speak I drown in the shadows.

....

from "Shadow"
–Diane M. Laboda

The day she died

I cracked eggs in the kitchen and the kids
watched cartoons, a box
of cereal between them, the dog
at their feet, waiting.
Onions sizzled and the yolks,
they swirled around the luminous slices.

November, fog clung to the bay,
as I drove over the bridge, past the salt flats,
stretched and under-shining in the dull light.

The metal shoulders let down, she lay
in the bed in the middle of the living room.
We washed her stem-thin arms, her boney
chest, child-like legs with cool bowls of water,
white cloths. Penelope began to sing.
The *sh'ma* at first, then kirtans. We praised.
We washed and sang, low and slow,
moved as one great bird over her body.
Stacy blew-dry her hair. Kathleena patted on
foundation, rouged her lips, whisped on black
mascara. We pulled up the sheets, tucking

whiteness around the tiny mound of her.
Lynnie pulled out rose petals and, still singing,
we fluttered them, spreading around our Baba Lu,
a canopy, peace and peace and, again, peace.

....

–Tina Cervin

April 3, 2017

My father has always had an incredibly strong life force—one always felt that hearing him sing, especially, the deep and resonant largeness of his voice—and on my last few visits, I've felt something in him was working especially hard, past the vitality of his own body, to let go. On the last afternoon before my flight home (my sister having arrived to continue our vigil), I stood over my father's hospital bed and gazed at his sleeping face. He'd barely stirred at all while we were in the room, but nevertheless I felt a firm and clear communication reach me: "It's alright. It's time." And then, just behind it, "I love you."

I thought it would be hard to get on that plane, that everything in me would push against departure. But in truth, I knew that wherever my father was going next, I could not accompany him there. And—and this is the truth of it—I did not need to be with him to be...with him. As the plane rose in the sky, a thin line of orange came into view. The first inklings of sunrise. A new day, waking into itself, and everything it would bring—sadness, loss, beauty, courage, love, hope, surrender, stillness, life, death. There was nothing I could do to stop any of it, and there was no need. The current was moving and the only thing to do was move with it.

He is still here, sleeping mostly, and has for the past few days received many visitors who have come to be with him, perhaps for the last time. Members of the choir he directed, singing to him bedside. My uncle sent recordings of the Yiddish trio my father founded years ago, and my sister tells me he's listened to these many times, with a smile on his lips and in his eyes. Messages have come from every corner of the world, carrying words of support and friendship and love, and my sister reads each of these to him, and he listens. My brother is on his way tonight from Boston.

With only pain medication and IV fluids for hydration, my father is declining quickly, and I know that any day or hour, the phone will ring with news that will fell me at the knees and break my heart. There is no preparation to be made, nor could there be. And yet, I've returned home with a new and vital tenderness, a recognition of how thin the veil is between us, and how powerful this porousness is. How it links our stories to each other. How it shoulders our unbearable grief and holds it steady. Like the wings of a plane rising into an impossibly large sky. Like a slim line of orange bringing us out of darkness into so much good light.

in the after

Before, it will feel like this: a watchfulness, a worrying, the shiver against time, a deepening
groove of the third eye, the body pulling itself through doorways and days, a bottomless
cup of coffee raised and lowered in a metronomic cadence that fails to keep your sadness
from advancing, the mirror revealing more shadows than light, and everything—
a cul-de-sac, a broken wine bottle, a pair of shoes flung across a highway median—
convulsing with metaphor. It will seem as if you've never been more alone or further away
from home, so when the call comes, you'll first mistake it for another wrongness, another wound,
the world broken from the spine of its axis. And it's true, it may be like that for a long while,
but in the after, swimming in the ether of your grief, a softness will graze at the back of your neck,
like the hand you placed at the back of his those last days, and where you know it will rest forever.

–Maya Stein

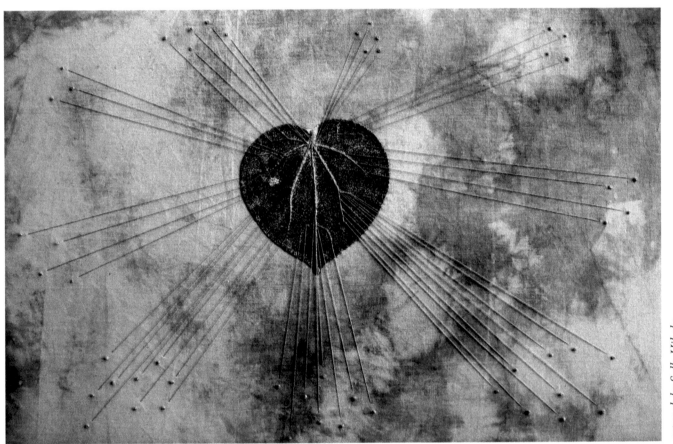

artwork by Sally Hikaka

CONTRIBUTORS

Allison Downey is a storyteller, singer-songwriter, educator, and speaker who believes in the power of story and song to inspire, foster connections, and teach us about ourselves. With an MFA in theatre, Allison has performed at such prestigious venues as The National Storytelling Festival, The Moth Mainstage and on Michigan Radio (NPR) as co-producer, host, and creator of the award-winning storytelling program, "The Living Room." Her musical CDs have garnered awards and radio play in five countries. A professor at Western Michigan University, Downey offers keynotes, workshops, retreats, courses and coaching in creativity, personal narrative and organizational storytelling. Allison is currently writing a book about her recent tangle with cancer. She's happy to be here.

Amy Tingle has been a visual artist and a writer since she can remember. In 2010, sensing a need in her community to make creative expression more accessible, Amy founded BraveGirlsArt, a series of art and self-empowerment workshops and camps for girls and women. Since then, she published a book of her writing and collages, *Strange Diary, or How to Make a Collage*, and has exhibited her work in galleries throughout the United States. She also co-founded a small business, The Creativity Caravan, with her wife, Maya Stein. You can find Amy on Instagram as @tingle and on her website, amytingle.com.

Anjika Grinager is a graphic designer and amateur philosopher who recently relocated to Portland, Oregon after raising two amazing boys in Santa Cruz, California. When she's not creating intuitive designs for her clients, she self-medicates with writing.

Anne-Claire Bonneau French. 36. Born in Paris. Ex-copywriter. Now living in Bordeaux. In love with the English language. She writes, "What can I say in a short bio that could convey who I am and how I experience this life and this world? I write because I have always felt called to write. To testify to the beauty and pain of being human. Now I'm trying to share my words with the world, hoping they can resonate with others' experience."

Annette Januzzi Wick is a writer, blogger and author of *I'll Have Some of Yours: What my mother taught me about dementia, cookies, music, the outside and how to find the best care home.* Her writings have appeared in the Alzheimer's Association Cornerstone, *Grief Becomes You*, Erma Bombeck Humor Blog and *Movers and Makers*, and have received awards from Writer's Digest, National Society of Newspaper Columnists and USA Book News. Annette and her husband make their home in a historic neighborhood in Cincinnati, Ohio. annettejwick.com

Brandie Sellers Counselor. Writer. Teacher. Brandie counsels cancer survivors and others who have experienced medical trauma, and adults experiencing life transitions. Brandie became a counselor after she completed treatment for breast cancer so she can support other people to overcome their struggles. In addition to counseling, Brandie has been teaching yoga and Ayurveda since 2005, and is a Registered Yoga Teacher at the 500-hour level with Yoga Alliance. She has written for cancerwise.org, and speaks to cancer survivors, counselors, and other professionals about cancer survivorship. Brandie is crazy about her three children and living an artful life with big adventures.

Candida Maurer PhD, is a mind-body-spirit psychologist who along with her husband, Michael Santangelo, PhD, created Iowa's first integrative medicine center in 1996. It is still going strong today (eastwindhealing.com). When Michael became mortally ill, they encountered the biggest challenge to their spiritual devotion and growth that either had ever known. Held deeply by spirit, "Laying Out the Body" is the story of their last moments and hours together. Candida is currently finishing the book about their journey through dying and death, *Enlightenment on the Path of Grief*, an expansion of her blog by the same name (enlightenmentonthepathofgrief.com).

Caren Stewart is an artist, writer, and educator who has worked in a helping profession for 15 years, most recently as a counselor, focusing on clients experiencing domestic and sexual violence. Caren works one-on-one with clients, groups, and also workshops around the psychology of trauma, characteristics of domestic violence relationships, and building resilience and emotional regulation in survivors. She completed a Bachelor's of Fine Arts in sculpture and a Master's in Education and uses art and writing processes in her work with clients. Caren is also a certified Soul Collage® Facilitator.

Carol Mikoda teaches writing and new teachers in upstate New York. Some of her work has appeared in *Children, Churches, & Daddies* and *Acta Victoriana*. She lives in the country, where she walks in the woods or lies down on the grass to study the sky and photograph clouds or treetops. She also sings and plays bass guitar as often as possible. Although she enjoys travel, her cat, Zen Li Shou, would rather she stayed home. She blogs at starwatchersguide.blogspot.com.

Carolyn Sargent was born and raised in Perrysburg Ohio, where she married and raised a family after completing a BA in French at Otterbein College (now University); a junior year abroad in Strasbourg France created a deeper love of all things French as well as friendships that endure. Carolyn now lives just north of Orlando, Florida. In 2007, she completed a three year-formation experience (Audire) culminating in certification as a Spiritual Director, a profession she continues to practice. She writes, "For as long as I can remember, writing in one form or another has been another thread I hold on to."

Celeste Tibbets is a retired librarian who lives in Tallahassee, Florida.

Chris Gutjahr writes, "Photography is my way of expressing a moment without words, although I am using words now. Some people say, 'I want to remember her as she was, not as she is now.' I wanted to remember my love, Cathy, in all her aspects, including death. On her last day, Cathy's friends gathered around her bed. One at a time each friend came up to her to say goodbye. Even though Cathy had little strength, she embraced each with a moment of deep regard."

Christina Tran makes tender, autobio comics and essays that pull us toward a more compassionate world. She has been making webcomics since 2014 and self-publishing zines since 2015. Her artmaking is influenced by her backgrounds in design, teaching, and community work. Find her online at sodelightful.com or in-person at the renegade community art space called Mt. Caz in Corvallis, Oregon.

Cynthia Lee discovered herself as an artist later in life while raising nine children. Her education was claimed from the in-between moments. She is self taught at the school of chasing curiosity, exploration, and deep belief in the power of story. With a vibrant visual journaling practice that informs her voice, she has been creating mixed media artwork since 2011. Whether writing, painting, or creating side by side with others, her work is about inspiring women to trust their own inner wisdom. She carries with her the grief of the death of her 20-year-old son in 2017.

Dana Schwartz lives in New Hope, Pennsylvania. She has published short stories and essays in literary journals and anthologies, and was a contest finalist in *Crab Orchard Review*, *New South*, and *Juncture*. In 2015 and 2017, her essays about motherhood were included in Lehigh Valley's "Listen to Your Mother" performances. You can find more of her writing on her blog, danaschwartzwrites.com. She is currently working on a memoir about motherhood and grief.

David Rosenheim is an executive coach and professional songwriter. He lives in a solar-powered house by the sea with his wife and two boys. The Weather Band, Hugh, and Winchester Revival have released his songs on seven critically lauded records, and his poetry has been published in journals including *Frigg* and *Common Ground*. David is a graduate of Oxford University and host of the Sustainability Leaders Podcast. davidrosenheim.com

Diane M. Laboda is a former teacher-librarian and retired Washtenaw Community College executive assistant. She enjoys exploring life's mysteries and sharing with others in her writing and artwork. She has published poetry, short stories and articles in *Huron Winds*, *Watermark*, *Lighter Breezes*, Project Grow's *Community Gardener*, *Cra.sh* online literary magazine, *Third Wednesday* literary journal, *Zoetic Press WLYA 2018*, WCC's *E-Link*, *Washtenaw Voice*, *OP/T Connection*, *Gallery One Colors & Voices*, issues 1-18 of *The Huron River Review*, *Blood Orange*, *The Big Window Review* and *Poetry Club* anthologies. She has published two chapbooks, *Facing the Mirror* and *This Poet's Journey,* and is working on her first book-length collection of poetry on caregiving and grief.

Elisabeth Reed Originally from Chapel Hill, North Carolina, Elisabeth Marshall Reed holds degrees from the North Carolina School of the Arts, Oberlin Conservatory, the Eastman School of Music, and Indiana University. Currently, she teaches viola da gamba and Baroque cello at the San Francisco Conservatory of Music and the University of California, Berkeley, and she has given master classes at the Juilliard School, the Shanghai Conservatory and the Royal Academy of Music. She can be heard on the Virgin Classics and Naxos recording labels and on the "Voices of Music" YouTube channel. A Guild-certified practitioner of the Feldenkrais Method, she specializes in working with performers. elisabethreed.com, voicesofmusic.org/videos.html

elizabeth claverie writes, "i have dabbled in wordsmithing since i was very young. I have been published a fair amount over the years; relative to the amount of work i have submitted; i mostly enjoy the writing. since i retired two years ago from teaching the art of language to middle schoolers, i have built a small artisan cheese following and i make cheese. this fall, i will be on the camino de santiago for the fourth time; hoping to write a book when i am finished. (and hoping to finish)."

Ellen McCarthy began writing poetry after she retired as journalist/ PR professional. She writes, "Poetry feels to me like commiseration, like talking to a friend. My husband died in 2015 after an 18-month battle with kidney failure. That same year, my brother died and my sister was diagnosed with cancer. I am not the same person I was in 2015. My heart now moves in and out of grief and gratitude. I take nothing for granted." poemsfromthebottomofmyanxiousheart.blogspot.com

Evelyn Donato is a published author, keynote speaker, and development consultant who works with non-profit organizations to help them increase their capital campaigns and program goals. She also works as an advocate for those living with invisible illness and chronic pain. Her blog "You Don't Look Sick" focuses on bringing a more informed awareness of the various challenges and misconceptions that those living with chronic illness and pain experience in our current culture. youdontlooksickblog.com

Gloria Lodato Wilson lives in New York City and is a Professor at Hofstra University, New York. Her academic writing includes numerous journal articles and book chapters on addressing the learning needs of students with disabilities. She is the lead author of *Teaching in Tandem: Effective Co-Teaching in the Inclusive Classroom*. Gloria's non-academic writing focus is primarily first-person short works and she is the author of *Confessions of a Praying Atheist*, a collection of vignettes which more or less follow her path through love, grief and life. Other works appear in various anthologies. Gloria enjoys exploring New York City, traveling and hiking.

Jennifer Glossop was born in England, raised in Chicago, and has lived the majority of her life in Toronto. Most of her career has been spent as a book editor with a particular interest in fiction. In the 1990s, she also started writing children's books, most recently *The Kids Book of World Religions*. Semi-retirement has brought time for other pursuits, including painting and travel. Grief came into Jennifer's life in a decade of losses: first of her father, then her only uncle, her mother, her husband, and her first grandchild at age 12. "My Old Purse" is about two of those losses.

Jennifer New is a living being who leads somatic inquiries, writes from the heart, works to keep up a house for two kids and two furry creatures, and dreams of the golden light of northern California.

Jess Larsen Brennan is the founder of Held Massage Therapy, a restorative practice that specializes in nurturing bodywork for challenging times in life. Her practice is influenced by Jess' 15-year career as a birth and death doula, childbirth educator and midwives' assistant. In addition to being a licensed massage therapist, Jess also has a professional background in public relations and communications, with a particular focus on supporting small women-owned businesses. She lives and works with her family in Montclair, New Jersey.

Kelly Albers is a full-time Mom to two beautiful children. She holds a Bachelor's Degree in Nursing and is also a Certified Legal Nurse Consultant. Kelly is a freelance writer and a published contributor in *Still Standing* magazine. She is currently working on a submission for *The Resilience of Being* anthology. Outside of creative writing work, she enjoys spending time with her family, photography and walks in the woods.

Laura Hoffman lives in Montclair, New Jersey with her husband, her teenage daughter, her 97-year-old mother and her two-year-old Corgi. She is a professional sign language interpreter and plays in a few rock bands around town.

Lisa Prantl A life in words. From childhood rhymes to free verse, block letters to keyboards, writing has been an ebb and flow in how to understand and live life for Lisa. When her son died, grief became a way of life, and writing about it opened a new understanding of death and the internal rhythm of grieving. That loss also led Lisa to train as a death midwife, with particular interest in home funerals and green burial. Lisa is a writer / facilitator at Women Writing for (a) Change in Cincinnati, Ohio, and a member of the Cincinnati End of Life Collaborative.

Lynn Bechtel is a writer, editor, gardener, reader, occasional knitter, and novice meditator. She grew up in Ohio but has lived in New England for most of her adult life. She writes essays and short stories. writeonharlow.com.

Margaret Todd Maitland explores the relationship between art and grief in her current project, *The Girl in the Fresco*, a memoir set in Italy. She has received numerous fellowships for her creative nonfiction as well as a listing in *Best American Essays (Notable Essays)*. As editor of *Ruminator Review*, she published interviews, essays, and book reviews by writers including Adrienne Rich, W. S. Merwin, Neil Gaiman, and Yoko Ono. She currently teaches creative nonfiction at The Loft Literary Center in Minneapolis.

Marie Louise St. Onge Marie Louise's writing has appeared in anthologies and literary magazines across the country including *Yankee Magazine*, *Clackamas Literary Review*, *Permafrost*, *Café Review*, and *Balancing Act 2*. She is the Executive Editor of *Ad Hoc Monadnock—A Literary Anthology*, a former editor for *The Worcester Review*, and a contributor to *French Class: French Canadian-American Writings on Identity, Culture and Place*. Marie Louise has read her poetry at universities, art and community centers, and bookstores throughout New England. She lives in Maine.

Meg Weber writes memoir, crafting true stories from her days. Meg's writing gives voice to how her life unfolds outside the boundaries prescribed for her. She writes about transgression, about edges, and about finding her way back into connection with her family through tragedy. Meg's writing is featured in *The Quotable*, *MUTHA Magazine*, *Manifest-Station*, *Rabble Lit*, and *HipMama*, and in anthologies by Seal Press, Sincyr Publishing, and forthcoming from Pact Press.

Michelle Harris is a Renaissance woman who writes and studies and paints and fixes leaking faucets and mows the yard and cooks and drives her kids to practice, all while listening to books and podcasts about living with intention and making the most of this one amazing life. You will likely find her organizing a closet or taking a long walk in the woods.

Naida D. Hyde Grown on Canadian soil, Naida became a nurse, psychiatric nursing clinical specialist, and psychologist, her specialty women's empowerment and healing incest wounds through feminist psychotherapy. She and life partner Helga Jacobson developed and ran a women's healing centre, RavenSpirit, focusing on shamanic healing for 15 years. Beginning at age 65, Naida worked/volunteered six times in Lesotho with girls, women and grandmothers. She has chosen daughters from Lesotho and a granddaughter, each the joy of her life. Audre Lorde and Raven are mentors. Naida's life imperatives are: Speak your truth. Never disappoint yourself. Make expansive choices. Give back. Love is all.

Nancy Gerber is a writer and psychoanalyst. Her books include *The Dancing Clock: Reflections on Family, Love, and Loss* (Shanti Arts Publishing, 2019); *A Way Out of Nowhere: Stories* (Big Table Publishing, 2018); and *Losing a Life: A Daughter's Memoir of Caregiving* (Hamilton Books, 2005). She received a Ph.D. in English from Rutgers University.

Pamela Graesser is a lifelong resident of New Hampshire and a practicing Psychotherapist for the last 34 years. She has a spouse, two cats, and an enormously wonderful group of female friends. She started writing when her mother was first diagnosed with Alzheimer's. She writes, "It became a way for me to process the disease and along the way; it became the therapy I needed to heal our relationship."

Patricia McKernon Runkle has worked as a writer and editor; she has also written songs and collaborative choral pieces. Her poems have been published in *Journal of New Jersey Poets*, *Paterson Literary Review*, and other literary magazines, including haiku journals. Her memoir, *Grief's Compass: Walking the Wilderness with Emily Dickinson*, was published by Apprentice

House Press (2017); it received a 2017 Nautilus Book Awards Silver Medal for lyrical prose and was short-listed for the Rubery Book Award. She lives with her husband in the New York area, and they cherish their two grown children. griefscompass.com

Rachel Weishaar is a mother of three, a writer, and amateur photographer from the St. Louis area. She loves to document beauty, even in decay. Photography allows her to record proof of peace, surrender, and solitude in a busy world.

Randi Stein is a mother and grandmother, visual artist, and dance/ movement therapist. She lives in Amherst, Mass. Now that she is 71, she is expecting to witness more friends departing. And she's not looking forward to that.

Raye Hendrickson Writing allows Raye Hendrickson to inhabit the inner workings of our bodies and spirit, and the outer reaches of space. Her poems explore the intricacies of relationships, and the mysteries and curiosities of science and nature. Saskatchewan's terrain allows her to breathe, and she is glad to be a prairie native. She lives in Regina, and loves being a massage therapist. Her first book of poetry, *Five Red Sentries*, was released by Thistledown Press in May 2019.

S. Miria Jo grew up (mostly) in New Hampshire. She lived and worked in New England until 2004, when she drove cross-country in a blue Chevy Blazer with her shiba inu and settled in Los Angeles. In 2017, she flew back and forth between the west coast and the east coast many times, to help her father downsize, pack, and move, and also help him with his serious medical issues. He passed away on October 27, 2017. The photographs that appear in *Grief Becomes You* were taken during a final trip back to New Hampshire, to sort and give away some special items to friends. miriadesign.com

Sally Hikaka is a Māori fibre artist living and creating in Aotearoa/ New Zealand. She writes, "As an indigenous artist I have a deep connection, love and respect for the natural world. I am drawn to botanicals, particularly New Zealand natives and use plant based materials in my work. My science background informs my process, influences my methodology and affords me valuable insights. I live and create in the space which exists at the intersection of my Maori and non-Maori ancestry, combining traditional techniques and materials in new and innovative ways. My current work explores people's emotional needs, perceptions and connections to place." pirihirajames.com, instagram.com/sallyhikaka

Sarah Greene Reed is a multimedia artist living in Austin, Texas. She holds degrees from the North Carolina School of the Arts, Rhode Island School of Design, and Sotheby's Institute in New York. Additionally, she studied at Parsons School of Design, the SPEOS Institute in Paris, and the University of Houston. Sarah's artwork has been exhibited internationally and is in collections such as The Museum of Fine Art, Houston, The Ogden Museum of Southern Art, The Morris Museum of Art, AT&T and the Capital One Corporate Headquarters. Commercially, her work has been purchased by the FX Network and Columbia Pictures. sarahgreenereed.com

Sarah Kilch Gaffney is a writer, brain injury advocate, and homemade caramel aficionado. She lives with her family in Maine, and you can find her work at sarahkilchgaffney.com.

Shannon Loucks is a spinner of tales, seeker of sunsets and director of adventure. Since as long ago as she can remember, putting words to paper has helped her make sense of the world. Whether it be to profess her love or untangle heartbreak leaking ink on to nearby surfaces has brought about both strength and courage. Much of her writing can be found at breakingdaylight.org. Her latest book *Love More*, is available through Amazon with a side project, *Caught In a Story*, that lives both on Instagram and Facebook.

Shannon MacFarlane lives, loves, and plays in the Pacific Northwest with her husband, son, and animal family. She walks with grieving families to preserve legacies and tell stories through photography, paint, and words and believes that art and grief (and love) are a natural partnership. Her work with families that include non-human members is under Slobbered Lens. She works with other families by referral only.

Sherry Jennings spent over 40 years living through the seasons with young children as an early childhood teacher while hoping a writer would emerge one day. When she retired three years ago, Sherry joined a writing group. Since then she has been excitedly putting her purple pen to paper writing poetry, personal essays and is currently working on a memoir.

Sondra Hall loves words as much as she loves bread (which is an awful lot) and enjoys galavanting around in her imagination with pencil and paper in hand. She wholeheartedly believes in the power of the written word to transform both writer and reader. Because she felt that kids didn't spend enough time swimming in their imaginations and applying their creative spark to the page, she founded "Take My Word For It!" as a way to bring the adventure that is writing to elementary- and middle-school kids. For 14 years, her organization served thousands of students in the San Francisco Bay Area, Boston, and northern Virginia. Her memoir-in-progress, *Admitted*, is an attempt to reconcile a hellish period in her and her young family's life, when she was swallowed whole by severe depression.

Sue Daly's poems have been published in several journals and anthologies. Her poetry chapbook, *A Voice at Last*, was published by DADs Desk Publishing in 2017. Sue writes "Plug into Poetry," a monthly newsletter highlighting Sacramento poetry readings and writing groups. She also leads a poetry workshop at Wellspring Women's Center in Sacramento. Sue has an interest in empowering women to write and share their poetry with others.

Susan Vespoli splits her time between Arizona and Washington state. She returned to school in her 50s to earn an MFA from Antioch University L.A. Her work has been published in *Nailed Magazine, Nasty Women Poets: An Unapologetic Anthology of Subversive Verse, Mom Egg Review, Emrys Journal, Writing Bloody, Role Reboot, New Verse News, Pact Press, South 85 Review, dancing girl press*, and others. susanvespoli.com

Tamara Bailie lives in Utah with her husband, three daughters, two cats, and one hedgehog. She is a songwriter and a poet and writes to help herself figure out how she feels about things.

Tanya Levy is a counselor, an educator, a writer and a digital artist. As an artist, she photographs nature, especially cloud hearts, light or whatever calls to be captured. Her photos speak to her and tell her their message. Her art is also featured in the *Priestesses of the New Earth* oracle card deck. She has worked in the human services field for 30 years. She is passionate about and a strong advocate for the healing power of everyone's own unique journey. Her writing can be found in the 365 book series created by Jodi Chapman and Dan Teck.

Teri Foltz began a career as a poet and playwright after retiring from teaching others to write. She published her first book of poems *Green and Dying* in 2017. She resides in northern

Kentucky, where she participates in several writing groups. She was one of 12 poets chosen to study with her favorite poet, Billy Collins in 2018. She is happy to be included in *Grief Becomes You*.

Theresa Proenza is an educator and nonprofit administrator from Vermilion, Ohio. Her creative writing includes narratives on family; reflections on life and the intersection of our public and private selves, the stranger within; and nature as a source of inspiration and guidance in life.

Tina Cervin is a poet, teacher and yogi who divides her time between San Francisco and Sonoma County. She has taught with California Poets in the Schools and has studied with Ellen Bass, Marie Howe, and Dorianne Laux, among others. She guides women in generative writing around her dining room table at Come to The Page. She co-edited *A Ghost at Heart's Edge: Poetry & Fiction on Adoption*.

Victoria Ostrer is 49-year-old dormant artist, pursuing a new career to be around animals. She writes, "I recently woke up and started actually living the life that I dreamt I was living!"

grief becomes you

ACKNOWLEDGEMENTS

Thank you to my family, and especially my mother, Randi, my sister, Mikhal, and my brother, Adam, for all the things that don't have words. Thank you to my nephew, Eli, and my niece, Teia, for the healing and hope they've given me, undoubtedly without knowing it.

Thank you to the circle of my father's friends who kept watch with me in France, particularly Ian and Glenys and Monique and Mary and Jean-Claude and Corinne and Magali. Thank you to Stan and Bob for the weekly check-ins from California. Thank you to Claudine, who arrived at the crucial moments. And thank you to Sue, who lent me a bicycle and a map and a cell phone, whose steady concern and care became a lifeline, and who has kept a piece of my father alive in her garden.

Thank you to Rowena, for fielding that first anxious phone call and for holding the ground firm.

Thank you to Peggy, for the offer of a plane ticket, her invaluable guidance, and her indelible kindness and love.

Thank you to the UNs, for filling in the empty spaces always, and for being such divinely good friends all these years. And good God, for making me laugh.

Thank you to my writing girls, who knew what to say and said it beautifully, and in whose strong and gentle company I have always felt held and fed.

Thank you to everyone who leaned in and listened while I wrote in an old stone house 3,000 miles away from home.

Thank you to all those who shared your story with me, who sent photographs and artwork, who stepped forward to say, "Here I am."

Thank you to Liz Kalloch for her gentle eye and firm grip, the dotting of i's and such, and that walk in San Rafael up the big hill that offered the prescriptive permission slip to be exactly who and where I was, without apology.

Thank you to the boys, Evan and Charlie, for saving my father's letters, and for loving him, and for loving me.

And thank you to my needle in a haystack, Amy Tingle, for knowing exactly what to do, and when, and for taking such exquisitely good care of my heart.

Maya Stein is a poet, essayist, writing facilitator, and itinerant photographer. Her work has been published in *Huffington Post, Alimentum, Taproot, Stone Gathering, Prime Number, Little Patuxent Review,* and other print and online literary journals. She has self-published two collections of poetry, two collections of personal essays, a series of writing prompt guides, and has maintained a weekly email poetry practice, "10-Line Tuesday," since 2005. She can be found online at mayastein.com.